AF712475

SHEPARD HILLS SCHOOL LIBRARY
9701 S. SHEPARD HILLS DRIVE
OAK CREEK, WIS. 53154

THE O.J. SIMPSON STORY

THE O. J. Simpson STORY

BORN TO RUN

LARRY FOX

Introduction by WEEB EWBANK

ILLUSTRATED

DODD, MEAD & COMPANY
NEW YORK

Copyright © 1974 by Larry Fox

All rights reserved

No part of this book may be reproduced in any form without permission in writing from the publisher

ISBN: 0–396–07009–4
Library of Congress Catalog Card Number: 74–7769

Printed in the United States of America
by The Cornwall Press, Inc., Cornwall, N.Y.

To Jack Horrigan,
our friend

INTRODUCTION

by Weeb Ewbank

Vice President, former Head Coach, New York Jets

The first time I ever saw O.J. Simpson play was in the Rose Bowl against Indiana, and I remember thinking then "what a great runner this is." The thing that's impressed me most about him since that day is the fact that he's been able to keep his feet on the ground off the field. When I was coaching against him, he'd always make it a point to come over before the game to shake hands, and I like the way he always gives his line full credit after he's had a big day.

From talking to him and from watching him play, he's all you'd want in a football player, and in all my dealings with him he's impressed me as the kind of person you'd want your son to be.

As a running back he's got to rate with Gale Sayers, Jim Brown, Red Grange, and those people. He doesn't have that long stride of the late Willie Gallimore, but he's got better balance. Lots of times he looks like he's going to the ground, but he'll get his hand out and run along on all three for a while until he's righted himself. When you watch O.J. on films, all you can do is applaud . . . and be glad he's not doing it to you.

Jim Brown would scare the hell out of you, too, but I'd rather try to defense Brown than Simpson. Jimmy was strong, and he'd tuck that shoulder in so you couldn't get hold of anything, but he didn't have that burst of speed O.J. has. The problem isn't to tackle O.J., it's to catch him.

Gale Sayers and O.J. are a lot alike in style. They both have great speed and run under control. But O.J. is a lot stronger than Sayers and, of course, has proved more durable. It's really something to carry the ball as many times as he did in his record year and not miss a game.

The thing that makes O.J. so durable is not only his strength but the fact that you never get a good shot at him. He's got great peripheral vision, which enables him to spot tacklers and run for that daylight. Also, his speed scares a lot of tacklers. You've got to be sure when you're tackling him. You don't see many teams really trying to go after him and hurt him, because if you did, he'd really tear you apart. It's a rarity when one man brings him down. He doesn't break tackles with his power like a Larry Csonka or Steve Van Buren or Jim Brown, but because he's a stop-and-go guy, and because he's always running under control until he sees that opening. Then he explodes and he's gone.

He and Red Grange are a lot alike, and I'm sure that before O.J. is done he'll have the same charisma as the Galloping Ghost. I saw Grange in college and as a pro, and I'll never forget one game he played against Ohio State when he was with Illinois. Ohio State was determined to stop Grange's wide end runs, so it seemed as if they had men spread out all over the field on defense. Well, Grange would just start out wide and then cut back over the middle, which is the same kind of thing that Simpson does so well, and he killed 'em. Red was a little huskier, but I don't think he was as fast as O.J. He was a great controlled runner, too, and, like Simpson, a fine receiver.

I never saw the Indian, Jim Thorpe, play, but I understand he was more the bruiser type, like Jim Brown and Csonka. Among the halfbacks you'd have to rate O.J. along with Sayers and Grange.

Myself and all of our players had mixed emotions when we faced O.J. as he was going for the record in the last game of the 1973 season, which also was my last game before I retired as head coach of the Jets. We all liked him personally and we thought he had worked hard and deserved to break Jim Brown's record. I said I hoped he made his needed 61 yards to pass Brown, but that he took 61 carries to do it, which, of course, wouldn't hurt our chances of winning the game.

As it turned out even though our defense was ready for all his favorite plays, he got considerably more than 61 yards and became the first back in pro history to gain more than 2,000 in a single season.

At the time I said it was no disgrace not to stop a back like O.J. Simpson, who will go down as one of the greatest who ever played, and I still feel the same way. That's because O.J. Simpson is a credit to the game off the field, too.

Contents

THE O.J. SIMPSON STORY

1

O.J.'s Way

The skies were darkening, the field was frozen, there was snow on the scruffy turf of New York's Shea Stadium. The date was December 16, 1973, final weekend of the National Football League season. The pairing: the Buffalo Bills against the New York Jets, two teams going nowhere. More than 47,000 fans were in the park, but almost 13,000 less than capacity on this miserable day.

In the visitors' huddle early in the fourth quarter of what had turned into a rout, a rookie quarterback named Joe Ferguson was conducting a countdown to glory.

"Okay, guys, I got something to fire you up," Ferguson proclaimed as the Bills' offense took the field for the final period. "The Juice only needs 60 more yards."

The other Bills didn't have to ask, "Sixty yards for what?" They knew.

Their star, O.J. Simpson, had come into this final game only 61 yards short of Jimmy Brown's record of 1,863 yards gained rushing in a single season. The record had stood impregnable for a decade. No other NFL running back had ever come close.

Starting out against the Jets, the Bills had given the ball to Simpson again and again. "That was our deal," Ferguson would say later. "We wanted to start out right away to see if we could get the yards for Juice . . . and then we'd try to win the ball game."

By the end of the first quarter, Simpson had his record. By the end of the half, Buffalo had the game in hand, leading 21–7 en route to a 34–14 walkover. But by mid-third quarter a new target came into view. One of O.J. Simpson's all-time professional goals had been to gain 2,000 yards in a single season, a total once believed to be unattainable. Now Joe Ferguson, on advice from the coaches who were getting a statistical recap from the press box, was telling Simpson he was only 60 yards away.

O.J. got even closer before the Bills gave up the ball, and it seemed that even New York fans begrudged the minutes Simpson had to mark time on his march to glory. A fan threw a snowball at Joe Namath (who threw it back), and the Jet offense obliged by continuing to be inept. They punted the ball away, and Simpson and his partners trotted out onto the field for what they knew might be their last offensive thrust.

Darting easily around right end despite the treacherous footing, Simpson picked up 22 yards. He hit left guard and was stopped for no gain, but then he turned the left corner and added nine. Jim Braxton, the Bills' crunching fullback, took over for two carries to give O.J. a breather and provide some distraction for the Jet defense. Then the Juice resumed his record assault. Sweeping left end, he gained five yards more, and now he was only four short of the elusive target.

As if by prearrangement, the Shea Stadium lights suddenly blazed on to provide a million candlepower backdrop for Simpson's record run. All through the drive, young Joe Ferguson had been keeping track of the yardage. "Okay, Juice only needs four more," he said as he clapped his hands to break the huddle, his steaming breath punctuating the words.

The Bills' linemen lumbered up to the line of scrimmage. Mike Montler hunched over the ball, and Ferguson stuck his palms under the big center's rump. He called the cadence. The play was a No. 5, in Buffalo terminology, straight power with the fullback, 243 pounds of Jim Braxton, leading the way outside the left tackle. J.D. Hill, the split end, was pulled in to provide a second tight end for more blocking power. All the Bills' wide receivers have to block.

The Jets had a blitz on. Rookie linebacker Bill Ferguson was supposed to hit into the off-tackle gap, but he was late coming up, and Hill turned him outside the play. Dave Foley, a former Jet who had been branded a failure before being shipped to Buffalo, was the left tackle. He drove Steve Thompson, the defensive tackle, to the inside, and here came Braxton leading the way and driving back the safety man. Joe Ferguson had taken the snap, whirled and slapped the ball into O.J.'s stomach. Almost gracefully, Simpson sent his 212 pounds careening into the line. He knew the hole would be there, and it was. By the time safety Phil Wise recovered and made the tackle, O.J. had run for seven yards. He had his record with three yards to spare. Two hundred yards for the day, 2,003 for the season.

"Was the hole big enough for you?" Braxton asked with a huge grin.

They had stopped the game earlier, when Simpson broke Jim Brown's record, and now they stopped it again. The referee handed O.J. the ball. His teammates threw their arms in the air in triumph, leaping and cheering like so many schoolboys. Then they hoisted O.J. Simpson onto their shoulders and carried him to the sidelines as the Juice, in exultation, brandished his fist in the air. When he reached the Bills' bench, Simpson, for the second time in the afternoon emotionally embraced his head coach, Lou Saban. It was Saban who had saved O.J.'s professional career.

The crowd, which had been pulling for Simpson on his record quest against the home team, cheered O.J.'s achievement as if he was one of their own and gave him a standing ovation when he left the field. The Bills were leading, 31–7, at this point, and less than six minutes (5:56 to be exact) remained to be played. No one begrudged Simpson his early leave to avoid a certain postgame mob scene.

The Jets had been overwhelmed all week with press requests to cover Simpson's record bid. They ended up issuing more media credentials than for any home game since the American Football League title playoff against Oakland in 1968. To accommodate all the writers and cameramen whom they knew would want to talk to O.J. after the game, the Jets set up a special interview room off the corridor deep in the catacombs below Shea Stadium.

As the Bills clomped off the field after the final gun, Simpson waited by the door. As each of his offensive teammates entered the dressing room, O.J. again congratulated and thanked them.

Budd Thallman, Buffalo's public relations director, was in the dressing room, too, anxious to escort Simpson to his interview. But O.J. refused to budge. "I'm not going in there without the rest of the guys," he said stubbornly.

Minutes later the sound of 11 pairs of cleats echoed off the concrete floor as Simpson and his Praetorian Guard stomped down the corridor to meet the press.

"I want to introduce the cats who've done the job for me all year," Simpson told the hundreds of reporters, and then he proceeded to recognize his ten teammates by name, adding a little personal line about each. He paused a moment extra at Reggie McKenzie, the huge guard from Michigan to whom he always refers as "my main man." It was McKenzie who had first planted the seed of a 2,000-yard season in Simpson's mind many months before . . . and who helped make it possible.

"I just want you to know I hope to stay in the league until all these guys get old," Simpson said, as he rolled his eyes in the direction of his hulking, grinning teammates. "That way, no young back can get behind them and break my records."

It was a touching and spontaneous gesture. With some players it might have been considered corny, but not with O.J. Simpson. His sincerity outshined even the white-hot television lights. This was O.J.'s way.

"He's a helluva man," McKenzie declared. "I mean, who

else do you know would take the entire line to a national press conference the way he did? He's just beautiful."

A little further down the hall, in the Jet dressing room, the loser's coach, Weeb Ewbank, was paying a tearful farewell to his players. This was his last game before retirement, and his team had just been soundly beaten. But there was less hurt than there might have been. Weeb Ewbank's entire life had been football, and he was fully aware that he and his team had just been a party to one of the game's greatest moments. "There's no disgrace in not stopping a back like that," he declared.

The Jets had geared their entire defense to stopping Simpson, who had carried the ball 34 times. They knew his record quest would not harm the Bills' offense because he was their offense.

Typical was the play on which Simpson actually broke Brown's record. The Bills had set their tight end, Paul Seymour, a converted tackle, to the left. Hill was in tight on the right, and Bob Chandler, the flanker, was in close on the left. The entire Jet defense was overshifted in this direction! The play was telegraphed, a "27," Simpson's favorite, sweeping left. Seymour blocked in on defensive end Mark Lomas, right guard Joe DeLamielleure pulled out to lead the interference, and Braxton, after taking a fake from Joe Ferguson, hit into the hole vacated by DeLamielleure.

The Jets were waiting, but O.J. still gained six yards; at that moment Jim Brown's record was erased from the book.

Later, perhaps on the plane home to California, O.J. Simpson had time to think about the years that had led up to this crowning achievement. He had to think back to his ghetto upbringing in a broken home in San Francisco; of the many times he could have taken the wrong turn in his life; and of the times when he did go wrong only to have some person or force intervene to save him for a worthwhile life.

"It seems as if there was always something or someone watching over me," he reflected one quiet afternoon. "To tell the truth, quite often I do ask, 'There obviously is something You want me to do. I just wish You'd tell me what it is.' "

As he ponders these fortunate turns, Simpson recalls another great run he once made, perhaps the most important run in his life. It wasn't on a football field. If he hadn't found the right hole then, there would have been no records, no press conference, no glory. The only numbers would have been those written across his chest in the prison file. His records would have been in the police station, not enshrined in the National Football League's Park Avenue offices.

It occurred when Simpson was a teen-ager, growing up on Potrero Hill, a warren of public housing. His mother and father were no longer living together and out of this broken home, Simpson emerged as the leader of his street gang, The Superiors.

Simpson already was street wise, and he knew that if you walked down a row of parked cars long enough, you'd find one with the key inside just itching to be stolen. Young O.J. had stolen cars before. It was cheaper than paying the carfare to go to a party. Afterward, Simpson and his cohorts would drive back to their neighborhood and abandon the car a few blocks from home.

This night, though, the car Simpson chose to borrow was equipped with a standard transmission, a stick shift. He'd never driven one before, though he'd seen it done. He knew about the gearshift and the clutch, and knew it was all a matter of timing—let up on the clutch, and then hit the gas as the gears mesh.

But driving the hilly streets of San Francisco requires a special touch. Even experienced drivers will stall out when they have to start on a steep upgrade. O.J. Simpson definitely was not experienced . . . and now he was scared, too. The motor had died as he was stopped for a red light, and a police car was pulling alongside.

Again and again he turned the ignition key to start. Again and again the motor faltered, then died as he tried to get it in gear. The police officer looked at Simpson suspiciously and started to get out of his car. At this, O.J.'s companions panicked. All the doors flew open, and out they went fleeing in all directions. Those black faces disappearing into the night were an admission of guilt in the ghetto. O.J. was in for it, but as the officer approached, almost miraculously the motor coughed into life, and Simpson raced off. Fortunately, the policeman had been riding solo in his squad car. He had to walk all the way back before he could give chase, and that gave Simpson time to squeal around the corner. But it wasn't enough time to get away, either. The policeman was in hot pursuit and around and around they went, two full turns around the block past historic Market Street.

Finally, O.J. got a little lead, turned a corner, slammed

on the brakes, and dashed off into a used car lot. As the police car turned into view, O.J. ducked down beneath the cars. His heart was pounding. Surely the policeman could hear it beat. Surely he could hear O.J.'s heavy breathing. The cold perspiration of fear stung his eyes. Beneath the cars Simpson could see the policeman's heavy-soled shoes and blue trouser legs, as he searched up and down the rows of cars.

For a moment the policeman turned his back as he headed up another aisle. Simpson seized the opportunity. There was a providential alley situated behind the used car lot. Using his sprinter's speed, he fled down the only escape route and ran up on a second-story balcony of a nearby apartment house.

Once again, Simpson threw himself to the floor, panting in panic. He saw the policeman make his way through the alley. "Please, God, don't let him look up," O.J. pleaded silently. Finally the officer left. O.J. heard him start up the squad car but, for what seemed like hours, he remained huddled on the balcony. He had to be sure the cop was gone. He prayed again that none of the householders would have reason to leave their apartments at this late hour and spot him on the balcony. A scream, another call for the police, and this black boy wouldn't escape again.

Finally, certain at last that the coast was clear, O.J. Simpson walked down the steps and returned home.

Describing the incident many years later, Simpson could laugh. "It was almost funny," he chuckled as he recalled his frightened companions scattering like quail and the wild chase around the block like something out of a Tom and Jerry cartoon.

"I guess you could say that run down the alley was the most important run I ever made," Simpson said seriously . . . but that was only part of the troubled ground O.J. Simpson would have to cover before he could acknowledge the screaming thousands at Shea Stadium on a freezing December afternoon.

2

Going Down Potrero Hill

They call it Potrero Hill. It's in San Francisco, and it's a nest of low-cost government housing. Most people say the ghetto of San Francisco is called Oakland, but this isn't altogether true. Small enclaves of blacks are spotted throughout San Francisco, and Potrero Hill is one of them.

On July 7, 1947, a son was born to James and Eunice Simpson, their third child and second boy (with another daughter to follow). As Mrs. Simpson would recall later, "He was a heavy baby, the fattest of my four."

It was an aunt who came up with the inspired name of Orenthal James for this newest Simpson, and to this day nobody is quite sure why. "She was always thinking up names like that for people in the family, and she stuck another nephew with the name of Gursel," O.J. moaned years later. "It wouldn't have been so bad, except when she finally had kids of her own she named them Stuart and James."

When Simpson was struggling to make it as a pro during his early days in Buffalo, columnist Bud Furillo asked

Sid Gillman about O.J. Gillman, former college and pro coach who now runs the Houston Oilers, replied without hesitation, "O.J. made it the day he was born. He was born to run."

Not quite true. O.J. Simpson, perhaps pro football's greatest runner, had trouble learning to walk. As he approached his first birthday, his mother became concerned and took the lad to see a doctor. There it was discovered that young O.J. was suffering from a calcium deficiency, something like rickets. He would have to wear braces on his legs for awhile.

In some respects kids in the ghetto are no different from those in affluent suburbia. They are just as cruel. Simpson was teased first for his braces and then, after he cast them off, for his skinny legs. Orenthal James had long since been discarded in favor of O.J. (With the Buffalo Bills he's known simply as Juice, an easier-on-the-tongue derivation of the O.J.-inspired "Orange Juice" that was seen in print more often than spoken.) For awhile O.J. was called Pencil Legs on Potrero Hill, and today his legs are still somewhat bowed. This, however, may have something to do with his development as a football player. Floyd Little, a great running back with the Denver Broncos, also has permanently bowed legs. "I stand 5-foot-10," he jokes, "but if you straightened my legs out, I'd probably be 6-foot-5."

Later, another portion of his anatomy led to a different name. His playmates referred to him as "Headquarters," not because he was particularly brainy or for his yet-undeveloped leadership qualities, but because his head seemed a little too big for his body. (This extralarge head would prove an embarrassment when he first signed with the Bills. For a few days he practiced bare-headed because they had no helmet to fit him.)

By the time O.J. was five years old, his parents had separated. Fortunately, his father, a bank custodian, continued to live in the area and remained somewhat of an influence, especially on the frequent occasions when discipline was required. But O.J. actually was raised by his mother, who also worked as a hospital orderly. "We never went without eating," O.J. remembers, "but there were a lot of people in our area who did. We knew what it was like."

One of the lasting memories of O.J.'s youth is of moving from one apartment to another. This would occur each time his mother received a slight raise in salary, or when one of the older children moved away. Each change in family or financial status would make the Simpsons ineligible for their particular government housing, and so they had to move. O.J. remembers that for some peculiar reason, as their fortunes supposedly improved with more money or fewer mouths to feed, the government housing for which they were eligible got worse. He still can't figure that one out.

Simpson's parents have two vivid impressions of their son in his early years. "It was always sports," Mrs. Simpson told sportswriter Dwight Chapin. And Jimmy Simpson recalls mostly his young son's boundless curiosity and ambition. O.J. liked to take his toys apart to see how they worked, but his father agrees, "Sports came first."

Sports is more than a game in the ghetto, and O.J., always intensely aware of the world around him, recognized this fact of life in a hurry.

"Everyone was rated by his athletic ability," he recalls. "If you were the best baseball player, you were the leader of the gang."

From the beginning there was this driving force within O.J. Simpson to be No. 1, to be the top man. The problem in his development was that it took him a long time to decide who or what he wanted to be and how best to go about it. He longed to achieve, but it's not easy in the ghetto to find proper goals. (In his first years as a pro, when the Buffalo Bills were an NFL "ghetto," Simpson says, "I tried to set goals for myself" even though his aimless team seemed to have none.)

But O.J. quickly realized that he possessed athletic skill, and that this was the route he would follow. "I was always," he says with forgivable pride, "the leader of the gang."

In the middle of the ghetto jungle was the clearing in which O.J. Simpson would sow the seeds for his escape. Atop Potrero Hill was a youth center with its clubhouse, basketball courts, baseball diamonds, and football field. It was here, almost like a young Moses going to the Mount, that O.J. made his commitment. He was not yet 10 years old.

O.J. remembers spending his first summers visiting relatives back in Louisiana. That's where he earned his first money, picking cucumbers. Later the family would visit an uncle, who ran a meat market in Las Vegas. Simpson remembers precisely the moment that his mother joined in his commitment to sport.

He was 10, and the family had just arrived in Las Vegas for a brief vacation. This may have been a respite for Eunice Simpson, but it spelled tragedy for her son. There was a midget league baseball game scheduled back home in two days, and O.J. was supposed to play. The little fellow was so unhappy and upset, he was ruining the vacation for everyone. So Eunice Simpson piled him into the car and drove the more than 500 miles back home so he could play. They arrived only minutes before the first pitch, and the commitment was forever sealed.

If you asked him and he took the time to think about it, O.J. could probably tell you how many hits he got that afternoon.

Before long young Simpson was playing all the games, including baseball with the older boys. ("I had to play with them, they'd beat me up if I didn't," he remembers with a chuckle.) By age 14, he was playing semipro ball with grown men. These were men who worked in the Hunters Point shipyards, and some had been professionals. Simpson, a catcher and relishing the position because of its take-charge role, led the team in hitting even though he was its youngest member. (He may have inherited some of this skill. Ernie Banks of the Chicago Cubs was a cousin of his mother.)

O.J.'s life soon became centered around the neighborhood house, and he still remembers "all the good playground directors, especially a man named Earl who got me playing chess and a lot of other games we never really knew about."

One summer he spent a few weks at Camp Mendocino in northern California. The camp was sponsored by a group of San Francisco businessmen called The Guardsmen, who collected money to send underprivileged kids away during the summer. O.J. was one of these, and today he still responds when The Guardsmen ask his help in raising funds.

By now O.J. was in junior high school and starting to run wild. There were fights, rock-throwing and truancy—the preamble to future difficulties as the ghetto closed in on this slim bright-eyed youngster. Eunice Simpson searched desperately for some way to get her son away from this environment.

At first it seemed as if she had found the means; then, in a moment of frivolity, her perverse son threw it all away. The coach of O.J.'s junior high baseball team also served on the staff at Saint Ignatius, a parochial high school with a strong athletic program. Impressed with O.J.'s potential, he promised Simpson an athletic scholarship when he finished junior high. But it was spring, and O.J. always has been a social fellow. The first dance party of the spring was scheduled at the neighborhood house, and O.J. skipped baseball practice to attend.

"I didn't think it was such an important thing, but, obviously, the coach did," Simpson says now. "He threw me off the team."

Not only that, the coach withdrew his promise of a scholarship to Saint Ignatius. One afternoon Eunice Simpson even went to the school to plead that her son be allowed back on the team. But the coach was firm, a junior high Vince Lombardi. O.J. would not play for him. "I learned a lesson," O.J. says today, grimly and with a trace of remembered bitterness.

Mrs. Simpson, a determined woman, refused to give in to the ghetto, however. In the normal course of events, O.J. would have attended Mission High School. All his friends went there, and the enrollment was mostly black and Mexican. But Eunice Simpson was not a woman to be denied. Somehow she managed to get O.J. enrolled in Galileo High in the North Beach section of San Francisco. He might have to ride a bus to get there, but that was good. Some of the old ties would be broken.

Once North Beach had been an Italian neighborhood. The DiMaggio brothers and basketball whiz Hank Luisetti had gone to school at Galileo. Now Chinatown was the dominant neighborhood, and most of the school population was Oriental, with some blacks and Italians.

And so O.J. Simpson made his first break from the ghetto, even though the cord was only stretched, not severed.

As he left the neighborhood for his first day at the new school, O.J. probably felt as he did the first time he came down from Potrero Hill to play flag football against a team from another recreation center.

"Until that day, I had always played against kids that I knew," he reminisced one day. "This was the first time I would be playing against kids I didn't know. I had no way of knowing how good they were. They were there waiting for us as we walked down to the other playground, and I remember the funny feeling I got in my stomach when I saw them in the distance."

"It's the same feeling," O.J. said, "that I get in my stomach now . . . every Sunday."

3

Years of Decision

When Orenthal James Simpson showed up at Galileo High School and went out for football, his first position with the freshman team was tackle. Tackle? Well, the assignment wasn't as incongruous as it might seem. Nearly 70 percent of the students at Galileo were Orientals. At 5-foot-10 and 160-pounds, O.J. Simpson looked like a member of the Chicago Bears among them. But, as his first coach, Jack McBride, recalls, "We made him a back the first time we saw him move."

By his sophomore season Simpson was a starter on the football varsity, and the next spring, after suffering a broken hand, he abandoned baseball for track.

Bob Sprenger, now publicity director for the Kansas City Chiefs, covered high school track for a San Francisco paper when O.J. was running, and he recalls one of Simpson's early flashes of maturity and sense of press relations.

It was at a city meet, and the team from Galileo had just broken a relay record. Sprenger was trying to interview the boys so he could get their names straight and maybe even write a little bit about them. But three of the four thought it was great fun jiving this reporter and giving him a lot of phony names . . . until Simpson stepped in. "Look, man, this guy's got a job to do," he chided his teammates, and Sprenger finally got his interview.

There were few records in football, however. Even on a team that included Simpson and his close friend, Al Cowlings, a big lineman who later would follow him to Southern Cal and on to Buffalo as a No. 1 draft choice, Galileo at one point lost something like 19 straight games. They didn't win, in fact, in three years.

When it came to football, Simpson's Oriental teammates were simply outweighed.

After three games of his senior year, Simpson's football career faced a major crisis. A new coach, Larry McInerney, had taken over that season, and he was unhappy with the team's progress. If he was going to revive the program, he felt that he might have to start over from scratch. Galileo's next game was against unbeaten Saint Ignatius, the school where Simpson had blown his scholarship chance some years before.

"If you guys don't win," McInerney warned the squad, "I'm going to bench all the seniors for good."

If McInerney had been forced to make good on his threat, the world might never have heard of O.J. Simpson, for football by now was the only motivating force in his life, the only reason he attended class at all. But, fortunately, Galileo won, with O.J. scoring three touchdowns on long runs, including one 90-yard gallop after he stole the ball from a Saint Ignatius player.

Simpson, however, says this game was not the real turning point in his high school football career—and thus his life. He says his closest call came a year earlier on the day of another important game, when Jack McBride caught him and Al Cowlings and some friends shooting dice in the lavatory. This was a suspension offense, and Simpson thought McBride would ignore the affair rather than risk losing two of his best players for the big game.

The boys were stunned when McBride said he was going to turn them in, and marched them into the office of the dean of students, a Mr. Smith.

"If you want something, you have to work for it and act like you deserve it. If you want respect, you're going to have to act respectable," McBride lectured the apprehensive teen-agers.

At the time as they were being led down the hall, Simpson was angry. Only later did he appreciate how McBride was willing to sacrifice a ball game and a small portion of his coaching ego to try to steer four black boys in the right direction. He would long remember the lesson, and it has become one of his favorite stories.

As they reached the office of the dean, the famous Simpson luck held true again. The other three boys went through the door first. O.J. held back a second and appeared to be walking in with McBride. The coach threw the confiscated dice down on the desk and said tersely, "I caught these guys shooting craps in the toilet." Then he turned to leave, but forgot to close the door.

The dean asked Simpson to close it, which O.J. started to do . . . from the outside. "Where are you going?"

"Oh, I wasn't with those guys, I was just helping Mr.

McBride bring them down," Simpson replied with an air of injured innocence that presaged his acting career.

McBride, of course, had already left.

"Well, if you need a pass to get back in class, pick one up from my secretary," the dean called out.

As his teammates rolled their eyes in silent disbelief and marveled at his smarts, O.J. Simpson escaped again and avoided what could have been a fatal suspension.

Yet, although he "got away with it" and played in the big game, Simpson has never forgotten McBride's integrity. He also says that if he had been suspended from the football team he would probably have quit school, returned to the streets, "and that would have been it for me."

This incident, of course, was pretty much routine for O.J. Simpson, boy troublemaker and gang leader of The Superiors.

There was the throwing rocks at buses, the shoplifting (after all, they were too young to *buy* beer and wine), the breaking up of parties, and, above all, the fights, the constant fights.

Once, as he talked of his youthful predilection for street fights, O.J. Simpson was asked if he ever thought of becoming a boxer. He disclosed that his uncle in Las Vegas, the one who ran the meat market, also trained fighters in that city, including a couple of small-time headliners. "He used to take me into the gym in the summers and asked if I wanted to be a fighter, but I said no. I couldn't be a fighter because I didn't like to get hit," Simpson recalled, his final words accompanied by a big grin, because they also describe his philosophy as a running back.

Fights were grounds for suspension, too, at Galileo, but again Simpson often found school authorities understanding. Brought in once for a midweek brawl on school grounds, he was told to take the rest of the week off "for a rest," in lieu of suspension.

"The dean liked me, maybe because he once coached football himself," Simpson mused on one occasion, "but I've always wondered just what it was that he saw in me—if he saw some potential in me and knew that if he just gave me the chance I would work it out. There were so many people like that when I was growing up. Time and time again I got away with things, and I thought it was because I was slick or smarter than the other kids. Like Al Cowlings, he got suspended five times in high school. I'd like to go back and ask some of those men why they always gave me another chance. But Mr. Smith, the dean, passed away last year. I'll never be able to ask him."

During these years, Simpson and his friends more than once spent the night in jail or in the juvenile center waiting for their parents to get them out of one scrape or another. Except for the car incidents, O.J. never did anything that would have brought him hard time. Unlike the stereotype Simpson says he and his friends found the ghetto cops understanding. It was only when they ventured outside into the white, middle-class neighborhood that police treatment became more severe. Often, though, he would be called as a witness when friends got into bad trouble.

One of these friends was Joe Bell, whom Simpson characteristically remembers for one slick move of going the other way and thus avoiding arrest after the others, at his suggestion, had stolen some wine for a party from a shopkeeper named Mr. Wu.

According to O.J. a San Francisco bus driver had once left "a piece of his razor" in the head of Joe Bell's brother after an altercation, and so Bell went after the driver and beat him up. This wasn't that serious an offense, but it was on Joe Bell's record when he subsequently was arrested for selling a marijuana cigarette to one of his high school teachers. The way O.J. tells the story, it sounds like a classic case of entrapment, but they called the kid "a pusher" and landed hard on him because of his record and because he refused to disclose where he had obtained the joint. This was 1965, and marijuana was real bad news then to the straight world. Joe Bell got two years in prison.

This story has a happy ending, though. While he was in prison, Bell saw a picture of O.J. Simpson, the college football star, in his newspaper. Bell was shocked, and this chance coincidence changed his life. "If he can make it, so can I," Joe Bell vowed, which also tells you something about O.J.'s high school reputation. After his release Bell went on to college to play football, and today he has an executive position in business. "He's got his own office and secretary and everything," marvels O.J., quite impressed in turn at these gold-plated symbols of All-American success.

As he grew older O.J. and his buddies became big fans of the San Francisco 49ers, and on Sundays they'd often climb the fence of Kezar Stadium to see the pro games. Afterward, they'd pick up some change by collecting seat cushions for the park concessionaire. He paid them a nickel apiece for each one they brought in.

This would take the boys an hour or two, and later they'd spend their new money at a nearby ice cream parlor. One Sunday the 49ers had just finished playing the Cleveland Browns, and who walked into the ice cream parlor but Mr. Cleveland Brown himself, the legendary fullback, Jim Brown.

"The other kids were really awed when he walked in, but, you know, I was the leader of the gang, and so I had to say something," Simpson recalled years later when his pursuit of Brown's records gave new meaning to the story.

"Jim Brown, you ain't so great," young O.J. jived, putting on his best swagger. "When I get to play pro ball, I'm gonna break all your records."

Brown just looked at the lad with a faint smile. "Well, you talk big now, but let's see what you do when you get the chance," he replied quietly.

Today O.J. Simpson points out with a laugh, "Now kids are always coming up to me just like that and saying they're going to break all my records, and so I tell them what Jim Brown told me."

The irony is not lost on the Juice.

Jim Brown, however, was not the most important celebrity to enter O.J.'s life during these troubled years.

It was another of those grim days as Simpson finished his high school years, teetering on what his wife later would call "the brink of disaster." O.J.'s father had just been called down once again to the Youth Guidance Center to get his wayward son out of trouble after a night in custody. James Simpson must have been shaking his head in frustration as he brought the boy back to his mother's apartment. But soon after they arrived, as Simpson recalls it, another man showed up. O.J. still doesn't know who he was or how or why everything was arranged. He's also a little unsure of the date, but he remembers vividly the stranger's invitation: "Come on, we're going to see Willie Mays."

Mays was then a starring outfielder for the San Francisco Giants, and as such was unabashedly referred to by Simpson as "my hero." However, O.J. and his companion didn't go to Candlestick Park but to Mays' own plush home in an exclusive section of San Francisco.

As they drove up Simpson had to notice the big cars in the driveway, and when they entered the house he was struck by the thick rugs, the paintings, the rich furnishings.

Mays was puttering around the house, and he didn't stop what he was doing as the awestruck teen-ager followed him about. He didn't ask Simpson if he'd been in jail or what he'd been doing to make this visit necessary, and O.J. was impressed at the lack of condescension . . . and also grateful that these embarrassing subjects could be avoided.

"Stay out of trouble," Mays told him. "Take care of your mother . . . Be fair to people . . . Do right."

Mays is not an exceptionally articulate man, and he actually spent some time telling this teen-ager to be good to fans and not to complain about signing autographs.

But in this case Willie's message was not so much in his words. It was in his achievements and what these achievements had brought him in the way of material goods. Years later Simpson would recall, "As we talked, I saw how much he had. When I realized that his philosophy had been so good for him, I knew it couldn't be all that bad for me."

It was perhaps at this moment that O.J. Simpson finally was turned to the straight life. He saw that an athlete could accumulate more worldly goods than the pimps and pushers of the ghetto.

The road to his own fancy house was not exactly a direct one, however. Again and again the hand of fate and coincidence . . . and of a determined mother . . . would have to reach in and guide O.J. Simpson.

The end of his senior season of high school football could have spelled the end of O.J. Simpson's education. There was no more sports incentive to remain in school, and many of his teammates dropped out right then. (One of these was Al Cowlings, which explains why Cowlings was a year behind O.J. at Southern Cal.) But Eunice Simpson insisted that her son hang in there and get his diploma. It was a crucial decision.

As he finished high school, making All-City for the first time his senior year, Simpson received inquiries from only one college, Arizona State, which never really followed up. One reason for this disinterest was the fact that O.J.'s team over the years had been spectacularly unsuccessful. The same was true of his academics. His grades may have been poor, but so was his choice of subjects. He never liked shop, and so his transcript included courses like homemaking (blush), the kind of subjects guidance counselors often load on ghetto kids to keep them eligible for sports and provide enough credits so they can be moved along out of the school system with a diploma. For some this is a benefit, for others who realize their potential late, a disaster.

Simpson learned his only chance to continue his education (and football) was through California's extensive junior college system. All summer he wavered between this alternative and joining the Army.

Some of O.J.'s friends had enrolled the year before at the two-year City College of San Francisco, and they were prevailing on Simpson to join them. They told him that he surely could win a place on the team on defense. O.J. today figures that this was because they themselves were running backs and feared his competition.

Finally, on the day before the deadline for matriculating, O.J. enrolled.

O.J. actually did start out playing defense at City, but by his second game the top running backs were injured, and he moved in. Although he continued to play defense, too, and played it brilliantly, offense would be his bag, especially after one game against San Jose City College, when he gained 304 yards on only 17 carries and scored six touchdowns. They came on runs of 88, 73, 58, 16, and 14 yards and a 27-yard pass from Bob Lee, later an NFL quarterback with Minnesota and Atlanta.

All the players on his team wore red and white helmets, but the only hat that fit O.J.'s unusually-shaped head was all white. Thus he stood out in more ways than one as he broke all the legendary Ollie Mattson's career school records in less than a season. With his white helmet, opponents knew when O.J. Simpson was coming at 'em, but there was little they could do about it as he gained 1,161 yards with an average of almost 10 yards a carry.

Simpson's 300-yard game won CCSF a bid to the improbably named Prune Bowl against high-powered Long Beach City. Long Beach, a 20-point favorite, featured such stars as Earl McCullouch and Mike Battle. Two Southern Cal assistant coaches, Marv Goux and Jim Stangeland, were there to scout them, but all they could see once the game commenced was O.J. Simpson and his white hat running wild with three touchdowns in a 40–20 upset victory.

Immediately after the game, the Trojan scouts made Simpson's acquaintance in the locker room. Goux, who had charge of the San Francisco area for recruiting purposes, promised that he'd be seeing O.J. again soon.

Dutch Elston, Simpson's coach, was aware of the visitors. "Southern Cal! That's where you want to go. That's big-time football," he told O.J. when Goux and Stangeland had departed.

An overture from Southern Cal was like a dream come true for the Juice, who had been taken with the school ever since 1963. He was a high school freshman then, not even playing varsity football, but he watched on television as Southern Cal beat Wisconsin, 42–37, in the Rose Bowl. At every game USC has a student dressed up in a Trojan costume who rides around the stadium on a white horse each time it scores. In a 42-point game Tommy Trojan got a lot of exposure and the display captivated young O.J. At that point the idea of actually attending Southern Cal was too remote even to be considered.

CCSF finished its season with an 8–1–1 record as O.J. scored a national junior college record—26 touchdowns. Now everybody wanted the use of his body. It seemed as if every four-year school in the country was trying to recruit him.

Simpson still wanted Southern Cal, though, especially after he visited the campus. This was during the pro football war, and players out of college were commanding huge bonus payments on signing contracts immediately after their final games. And on occasion, before. At some schools, like Arizona State, O.J. could see the new pros lounging around campus wearing alligator shoes and driving flashy big cars. At Southern Cal Mike Garrett had just signed a lucrative contract with the Kansas City Chiefs after winning the Heisman Trophy as the nation's top college player. But Garrett and the other newly rich Trojans still seemed like regular guys to Simpson, wearing their Levis and letterman jackets and hitching rides to class. O.J. liked the scene.

There was one little problem, however. Those homemaking courses just didn't carry much weight with the Southern Cal board of admissions. O.J. had made up a lot of his high school grade deficiencies in his first year at junior college, but he still needed a few extra courses like geometry to get into an academically esteemed four-year institution. Although Southern Cal couldn't bend its rules, there were many others who could and would. Pressure began in earnest from Utah and Arizona State to get Simpson to transfer after one year. The pitch was simple.

"Why go back to junior college and take a chance on getting hurt?" the recruiters crooned. "That way you can end up with nothing. Sign with us now, and we'll guarantee you a degree no matter what."

The offers were tempting, especially those from other

schools that included such under-the-table emoluments as new cars and outright cash payments.

O.J. was confused, especially since he was convinced he had nothing to prove after shattering all those junior college records and making J.C. All-America. His mother, always a profound influence, also could not see why he didn't transfer. It would certainly ease the financial burden at home, and some of the offers included money payments to the family.

That spring there were scenes right out of Abbott and Costello as the vacillating Simpson was buffeted from one school to the other. At one point O.J. finally decided to enroll at Arizona State, and an assisant coach was assigned to escort him to the campus.

They got as far as the airport, O.J., his mother, his fiancé, Marguerite, and the Arizona State coach.

Here the stories begin to conflict. One account maintains that Utah heard about O.J.'s intentions and sent a scout to the airport to head him off. But O.J. recalls it as one of the accidents of fate that seemed to follow his footsteps more closely than any tacklers. He said Utah just happened to show up by coincidence and accidentally spotted the Simpson party having a bite when Arizona State had to go to the men's room.

When Arizona State returned to the table, he spotted Utah crashing his party, and a fierce argument ensued.

In the confusion O.J. and his family kind of slipped away and went home.

Soon after O.J. Simpson surfaced on the Utah campus in Salt Lake City, where he actually signed a letter of intent to enroll. That night he was interviewed on a local tele-

SHEPARD HILLS SCHOOL LIBRARY
9701 S. SHEPARD HILLS DRIVE
OAK CREEK, WIS. 53154

vision station, and the announcer asked O.J. if he had decided on a college.

"Yes, I'm going to Utah State," Simpson replied as the stunned announcer quickly corrected him.

"You mean Utah, don't you?"

"Oh, yeah, Utah," answered Simpson, who refers to himself in those days as "a confused young man," and who even now has trouble telling all those schools apart.

Again Simpson returned home, but to get his belongings in the few days before the start of spring practice. This time the persuasive Marv Goux intercepted him. Goux, emotional but tough-minded, got right to the point.

"Look, O.J., what do you really want to do?" Goux asked.

"Well, I really want to go to USC," the 18-year-old halfback replied, "but I also don't want to waste another year in junior college."

Goux looked Simpson right in the eye. "You really want to go to SC, but you're willing to settle for something you don't want. That's a shame," Goux said bluntly. "Well, I happen to feel that anything worth having is worth working and waiting for."

Goux's approach made sense, especially since Simpson by now knew he wanted to make a career of professional football, and he knew that Southern Cal would provide the coaching, competition and national publicity to best further that aim. He agreed to remain in junior college for another season to pick up the required courses for Southern Cal. (The lesson in self-discipline and determination also was not lost on O.J.)

Simpson later would agree that his decision to wait was

for the best in a pure football sense, too. With Al Cowlings now a teammate, O.J.'s second year in junior college was even better than the first. CCSF compiled a 9–1 record, and O.J. scored 28 touchdowns on 1,391 yards to break his own one-year national record. More important, he entered four-year competition with complete confidence in his abilities.

(Simpson also feels it was best that he had gone to junior college in the first place. During this period he developed good study habits, a trait conspicuously missing in high school, and he was able to avoid the often painful and demoralizing route of most freshmen who must spend a year as midweek cannon fodder for the varsity.)

O.J.'s enlistement at Southern Cal wasn't quite that simple, however. Simpson's second-year record merely increased the recruiting pressure as football factories all over the nation sought his services. The money offers soared, too . . . and they were awfully tempting for this child of the ghetto who now was thinking of getting married.

One night the telephone rang in the Simpson apartment.

"This is Tom Hamilton, and I'm the commissioner of the Pacific-Eight Conference," the strange voice said in introduction.

Hamilton, a retired admiral, congratulated Simpson on his fine record and then he got down to the purpose of his call. He told O.J. that he was aware of all the recruiting pressure he was undergoing, and then he pointed out ominously that Simpson should know that wherever he decided to enroll—especially if it was in the Far West area for which Hamilton could speak—he would be "investigated."

It seemed like a grim sort of gratuitous warning for a young kid, but it was done with a purpose, and Simpson appreciated it. Hamilton was telling Simpson not to be tempted by offers of cash and cars, because they would be searched out and discovered. If it was found out that he had been recruited illegally, there would be no college career. His year of waiting would have been wasted.

"Looking back, I've got to thank the guy for telling me all that," Simpson says. "I could have taken a little money, went to that college, and been suspended and never played. And, obviously, all that's ever happened to me stems from the last two years of my career at USC."

In the end it came down to a choice between California in nearby Berkeley and Southern Cal in Los Angeles. California recruiters told him he would be their school's first black superstar and that if he enrolled at Berkeley he would not have to compete against the reputation of the Trojans' great Heisman Trophy winner, Mike Garrett.

The pitch, of course, backfired, the same way O.J. resented remarks of other recruiters that Southern Cal had such a wealth of talent that he would never get to play.

All these recruiters reckoned without Simpson's tremendous competitive spirit, the drive that compels him to go all out to win even in table tennis against his wife. He wanted to compete against the best, he wanted to match his skills against Mike Garrett's records.

O.J. Simpson finally made up his mind that he would attend Southern Cal for the simplest of reasons. As he told a reporter friend, "It's the thing I wanted to do all along."

4

"I Want One of Those"

The day O.J. Simpson left San Francisco to enroll at the University of Southern California for the spring semester was the day that he finally broke his last ties with the ghetto. It had taken almost 20 years of his life to get away, but now, at last, he was free. Los Angeles would be his home and, to make it truly that, in June he added a wife.

Marguerite Whitley had known O.J. since they both were in high school, only first she was Al Cowlings' girl. Marguerite came from a respectable closely knit middle-class family. At the beginning she was repelled by the rowdy, exhuberant Simpson. "Frankly," she says, recalling those days, "O.J. was a pretty terrible person."

But, like so many others, she soon fell under the O.J. Simpson spell, becoming aware that underneath the rough veneer there was a sensitive worthwhile person struggling to escape. (It took a little longer for her parents to accept the match, especially when her fiancé told them he planned to support their darling daughter by playing football.)

During those early days at Southern Cal, the couple lived in a modest second-floor apartment just off the campus, and Marguerite worked evenings at the school library. O.J. would show up early each night to walk her home, and while he waited he would do his own lessons. The whole thing worked out well and enabled O.J. to get off to a good start scholastically. Their first child was born during his senior year.

The change of life and scene was a major turning point for O.J.

In the past he had always been on the go, never at home. Always the leader of the gang, he quickly had become aware that leadership included built-in responsibilities. "You always had to be ready to go," he recalled. "If you're gonna be the leader, you had to pay the price."

What he meant was that if someone suggested a party or stealing some hubcaps or any other type of fun or mischief, the gang leader had to answer the call and head the expedition. If he let the guys go off without him, he would abdicate his position and someone else would step in.

Only through marriage and by moving out of town was he able to break the pattern, a pattern he must have known could only end in disaster. It was almost with relief that he left his old world and, fortunately, he had Marguerite to help him make the trip.

Even as he enrolled in the spring of his sophomore year, Simpson was being billed in Los Angeles as the new Mike Garrett. But O.J. wasn't so sure. He didn't know if he would play running back, flanker, or even defense for the Trojans. He knew of many junior college hotshots who had flopped in four-year competition. He wondered if he would be one of those. John McKay, SC's dapper and quick-witted coach, was uncertain only about O.J.'s permanent position with the Trojans. But that's what spring football practice is for, and that's why Simpson didn't wait until the fall semester to transfer.

O.J.'s spring practice lasted seven days. That was all he needed.

A couple of days into the off-season training period, McKay turned to his assistants and announced quietly, "Well, I think it's time to see what we've got here."

The Trojans had a scrimmage planned, and McKay wanted to learn if his prize prospect had the durability required to play tailback. Tailback was the key position in McKay's I-formation offense. As the scrimmage began McKay whispered a few words to the quarterback, who nodded his understanding. O.J. Simpson trotted onto the field, and seven straight times the quarterback called his number, all of them on plays that required him to crash into the middle of the line. Seven straight times the ball was slapped into O.J. Simpson's belly, and seven straight times he cracked into the mass, scattering bodies as he drove forward. With each carry, he seemed to get stronger.

Finally McKay called a halt. He had wanted to see if O.J. "could take it inside," and he was awed the way the Juice just "busted people over backward." As a substitute took over to give Simpson a blow, McKay turned to an assistant coach and winked. O.J. Simpson was the goods. A few days later he was excused from the rest of spring practice to run track.

(With O.J. running the third leg, USC's 440-yard relay team set a world's record, and Simpson also placed in the

100 to help the school win the NCAA championship. He had run a 9.4 100 in junior college, and he repeated this clocking regularly at Southern Cal to win recognition as the fastest football player in Trojan history. He also ran a 9.3 before he was through. Pro football players generally are clocked for the 40-yard dash, and in college and pro, Simpson has covered the distance in 4.3 seconds. Is this fast? Well, pro coaches generally will double-check their stopwatches and are extremely skeptical any time a player claims to break 4.5. Weeb Ewbank, for example, as he discussed his thoughts for the introduction to this book didn't believe Simpson had ever done a 4.3 until he saw it on his old scouting reports of O.J. as a collegian.)

O.J. Simpson had walked on the campus a few months before virtually unknown except to the football coaching staff. But before he played his first game, everybody in town knew who he was . . . and what was expected of him.

Big things also were expected of the Trojans. McKay had assembled a powerful team, and at the end of the season no less than five players were picked off in the first round of the NFL draft—Ron Yary (the first player chosen in the whole draft, by Minnesota), Earl McCullouch (Detroit), Tim Rossovich (Philadelphia), Mike Hull (Chicago), and Mike Taylor (Pittsburgh). At least half a dozen other future pros were on the squad, which also may have been one of the most free-spirited in the nation. Included in the cast of characters was Rossovich, who once set himself on fire while he was with the Eagles; Chip Oliver, who later walked away from pro football to join a commune; and the glass-eating Mike Battle.

O.J., who likes a good time himself, in comparison was a sober citizen in this company.

The Trojans were scheduled to open their 1967 season at Washington State, and on his first play, Simpson gained 15 yards with a little swing pass. Later he scored his first college touchdown as the Trojans won easily, 49–0.

The next week, though, the opposition was a little tougher. The Trojans were matched against nationally ranked Texas, and this was to be O.J.'s first appearance before Los Angeles fans. The debut started out poorly. Simpson fumbled early in the first quarter, and the Longhorns marched right in for a 7–0 lead.

O.J., however, matched that touchdown with a two-yard scoring run, and later his quick feet helped set up another TD and a field goal in a 17–13 victory.

Simpson's stat line showed 158 yards on 30 carries, and afterward Texas coach Darrell Royal declared, "I hope we don't see anyone [the rest of the year] with more capabilities . . . and I don't think we will."

The O.J. express rolled on. The next week he gained 190 yards and even threw a touchdown pass as Southern Cal came from behind to beat tough Michigan State, 21–17. He threw another TD pass in a 30–0 rout of Stanford.

The Trojans resumed the intersectional schedule that had been one of their attractions for O.J. the following week with a visit to Notre Dame. Southern Cal hadn't won in South Bend since 1939, and the Fighting Irish, rated No. 1 in the polls, were 12-point favorites. Notre Dame led, 7–0, at halftime, but the Irish soon learned what all future Southern Cal foes would come to fear. O.J. Simpson was a second-half football player. Some sports writers foolishly suggested that O.J. often loafed during the first 30 minutes, but this was not the case. It's just that as the game progressed, O.J.'s incredible stamina became more of a factor. He grew stronger as his opponents wilted under the pressure. As they tired O.J. was able to find those little cracks in their defenses and exploit them for big gains.

A Southern Cal linebacker named Adrian Young, who appropriately happened to have been born in Dublin, Ireland, intercepted four Notre Dame passes, but it was O.J. Simpson who carried the day on offense.

The Irish fumbled away the second-half kickoff, and O.J. ran in the tying touchdown from the one. Then he broke loose around end for a 36-yard touchdown run and SC led, 14–7. Still in the third quarter, Simpson's runs helped position a 22-yard field goal and, finally, to cap his tremendous performance, Simpson circled left end for three yards and his third touchdown of the game in a 24–7 victory. Talk started immediately of a possible national championship for the Trojans.

Simpson had gone to Southern Cal because he wanted to play big-time football. A lot of guys do, but they flop in the spotlight. Notre Dame is one of college football's premier showcase opponents, and on this day O.J. proved he could handle the pressure. He gained 150 yards and carried the ball 38 times, which would be his high for the season. Later he related, "I'd hear them call my number, and I'd say to myself, 'Oh, Lord, not again,' but once I got the ball, instinct took over and somehow my legs would move."

Newsmen asked McKay why he used Simpson so often.

Even though O.J. was a well-built 200-pounder, wasn't he risking injury? Or something? McKay, one of college football's quip-masters, smiled. "He's not in a union, and so he can carry the ball as many times as we want him to," McKay replied. "Besides, I like to watch him run."

To which Notre Dame's sports information director, Roger Valdiserri, could only counter, "Simpson's nickname shouldn't be Orange Juice, the O.J. should stand for Oh, Jesus . . . as in Oh, Jesus, there he goes again!"

It was a lament many opponents would repeat as the season rolled along.

The next week Simpson's carries dropped to an even 30, but what he did on those carries defies belief . . . 235 yards plus two running touchdowns and a pass for another as USC broke open a 7–6 game with 16 points in the final period against Washington. Simpson's first touchdown in in the opening period had come on an 86-yard run, and he then came back to lead the late explosion even though he'd been relieved briefly earlier with leg cramps.

"He has a tendency to get them when he carries the ball 50 times," McKay said drily.

Asked about his thought's during Simpson's 86-yard run, McKay quipped, "I thought whoever recruited him was very intelligent."

The following week the Trojans were improbable 34-point favorites over Oregon. You wouldn't give that kind of spread to an old lady's home against the Miami Dolphins, and people who took the points came out ahead, but just barely. The final score was 28–6 as Southern Cal won its seventh straight, but it appeared to be a Pyrrhic victory. Four minutes into the third period, O.J. limped off the field with a sprained right instep.

The injury did not appear serious at the time, but the next day Simpson was on crutches, and McKay's good humor quickly deserted him. "I doubt he'll play much more football for us—if any—this season," McKay said pessimistically. "The doctors tell me he's out indefinitely. Right now he can't run and if he can't run, he can't help us."

McKay's glum appraisal turned out to be unjustified. Simpson missed only one game, but Southern Cal beat California easily without him. It would be the only game he ever missed in college.

The next week, though, the Trojans had to head up to Oregon State, a tougher foe. Earlier in the season the Beavers had beaten Purdue and tied UCLA when those schools were ranked second in the national polls, and on the eve of the Southern Cal game, Dee Andros, their rotund coach, proclaimed, "Let's stop messing with the No. 2s and bring on No. 1!"

The field came up muddy the day of the game, and while the off track may have kept O.J. from scoring, it certainly didn't slow him down. Simpson gained 188 yards on 33 carries, but the Beavers' defensive game plan kept him from breaking any long runs. In the second half, when he usually came on strong, O.J. began to feel the effects of his injury. "It only hurt a little, but mainly I was tired," he confessed, and Oregon State made a second-quarter field goal hold up for a 3–0 victory.

The loss ended Southern Cal's hopes for an undefeated season, but it wasn't fatal. The Trojans had one more game remaining in regular season against crosstown rival UCLA. The Bruins also had only one blot on their record, that earlier tie when they had played Oregon State, and this bitter intracity rivalry was fraught with significance. A national championship, a Pacific-Eight Conference title, and the Rose Bowl invitation all were at stake.

On top of this there was an individual duel to spice the cake. In his brief career Simpson not only had established himself as a bona fide All-American candidate but also as one of the leading contenders for the Heisman Trophy, awarded annually to the best college player in the nation. Though only a junior, he was receiving strong support around the country. His strongest rival was UCLA quarterback Gary Beban, a senior. They would fight it out before the many thousands in Los Angeles Coliseum, plus millions more looking in on television.

"I'd give 10 years of my life to play in that game," said Marv Goux, the coach who had recruited Simpson.

This was the emotion of the moment as game time approached and, for once, the contest lived up to the preamble.

UCLA scored first, but the Trojans retaliated in the first period, and in the second quarter O.J. took a pitchout from Steve Sogge and ran 13 yards for a go-ahead touchdown, dragging tacklers into the end zone with him for a 14–7 halftime lead.

Beban, playing despite sore ribs, was brilliant. As the second half began, he maneuvered the Bruins to a tying touchdown and, early in the fourth quarter, UCLA scored again. The extra point failed, but still the Bruins had a 20–14 lead with just under 11 minutes to protect it.

But now it was showdown time, and as the shadows lengthened, you could literally see O.J. Simpson pull himself together for the final push.

All year Simpson had followed the Jim Brown habit of catching a moment's breather on the ground after being tackled, but UCLA players had adopted a countering strategy. Each time after swatting O.J. to the turf, they would rush over with an outstretched hand to help him up. It was foxy gamesmanship in the sheep's clothing of good sport. The Bruins didn't want to give O.J. time to catch his breath.

O.J., however, had been thinking, too. Despite all his talk of "instinct," there is a cerebral side to his style. (Just listen to him sometime discussing NFL linebackers, for example.) He noticed the Bruins had been keying on him all game, reacting quickly to his every move. To counter this, he started aiming for the wrong hole when he took the handoff, but then he cut back quickly after the defense was committed. It was the beginning of a stutter-step style that would make his early years as a pro so difficult.

But this was college ball, and it seemed to be working (as it had worked for Red Grange against Ohio State), and Simpson rolled on past the 100-yard mark for the seventh time in nine games.

As they turned into the final minutes, the new Trojan quarterback Toby Page twice in a row called on Simpson for a disappointing net of two yards. Now it was third-and-eight at the SC 36. If the Trojans had to punt, UCLA could very well run the clock on its victory. Page glanced around in the huddle. His eyes searched Simpson's face for signs of fatigue. "He thinks I can't carry the ball a third straight time," O.J. said to himself as he tried to set his features in a grim mask of determination to convey the confidence that he could do just that.

In the huddle Page called a play that did not involve Simpson, but, as he crouched under the center, he changed his mind. "Twenty-three blast!" Page yelled to each side of the line as he added the secret code that signified this was a "live" audible.

"Oh-oh, that's me," Simpson thought to himself as his muscles inwardly tensed and he strained to avoid a tell-tale tipoff to the defense.

Page called the cadence, fed the ball to Simpson, and O.J. took off around end. Reversing his field as he passed the line of scrimmage, he sprinted 64 yards to the end zone ahead of panting Bruin defenders. SC added the extra point, then held on for the 21–20 victory, which also meant national and conference championships and the Rose Bowl invitation.

The Trojans went on to beat Indiana, 14–3, in the Rose Bowl with O.J. scoring both touchdowns to be named player of the game.

When Marv Goux went out recruiting, he always wore the ring symbolizing Southern Cal's 1962 national championship. "Biggest ring I ever saw," recalls the dazzled O.J., who remembers Goux promising him, "You'll wear one of these, too, someday."

Now Simpson would have one, plus such individual honors as the national rushing championship, a place in every all-America backfield and recognition as UPI's

Player of the Year. But, when it came to the Heisman Trophy, O.J. finished second to Gary Beban.

Beban had enjoyed a fine college career (he was a bust as a pro), but all agreed that his being a senior had made the difference. Many voters felt that Simpson, only a junior, could very well "wait til next year."

Simpson's friends tried to console him after Beban's selection, but O.J. would have none of this. "Look, things have turned out just fine," he told them. "This fall I didn't even know how good I was going to be in college. I just wanted to make the team, and here we've gone to the Rose Bowl and won the national championship, and I've led the country in rushing and made all-America. I'm just happy I finished second."

At the start of the season, still tense as he worried about the new competition, Simpson hadn't even thought Heisman Trophy.

But after the Rose Bowl he visited the home of Mike Garrett. In a place of honor, he spotted Garrett's Heisman Trophy. The trophy is a massive statue about a foot high in dark, brooding metal that exhudes strength. The figure is that of a running back.

O.J. gazed long at the trophy. For the first time it began to sink in how close he had come to winning . . . and how badly he wanted it.

Turning to Garrett, he nodded toward the trophy and vowed with uncharacteristic seriousness, "Hey, I want one of those suckers."

5

"He's the Man"

Life continued a thicket of temptation for O.J. Simpson as he approached his second and final season at Southern Cal, but by now he could shrug aside sirens who might have caused the younger or less mature to pause.

Following his sensational junior season, O.J. received an offer from the Montreal Alouettes of the Canadian League to turn pro immediately. They sent him a three-year contract worth $65,000.

O.J. did weigh the offer briefly, for two reasons. The first was the merger of the two professional leagues in this country, which signaled the end of the insane bidding war for college talent. The second had been the lesson of his foot injury of the year before. For the first time the Juice had been served notice of his own mortality. "You can't think 'injury' during a game. You have to run with abandon," he said then, "but now I know it can all end on one play."

Still, Simpson was able to keep his eye on the main chance, just as he had done when he rejected the call of the obscure football factories after his first season in junior college. (Whenever he thought O.J. needed bringing down to earth, Marv Goux reminded him how close he had come to gaining all his yardage unsung in the media wilderness of Utah or Arizona.)

Simpson knew the big money and recognition would have to come on the U.S. side of the border, and so, without regrets, he rejected the Canadian offer. However, he retained the blank contract for his scrapbook. "If I never make it to the pros," he said, thinking of the possibility of senior year injury, "I can always show people what could have been."

Football at Southern Cal meant national ratings, the big intersectional schedule, television exposure, the Rose Bowl. Opening game is important in this context, because it sets position in the first weekly national polls. A team may spend the rest of the season struggling uphill to overcome the handicap of an opening defeat. The Heisman Trophy also is decided by popular vote (of newsmen and broadcasters) and here, too, junior year and early senior performance is critical.

The Trojans had suffered devastating graduation losses after their Rose Bowl victory over Indiana, but opponents were not impressed because the big man still remained. "Give me O.J. Simpson and 10 cheerleaders, and we'll meet all comers, from Green Bay on down," declared Ray Willsey of California. Still, there was no question Southern Cal's squad would be weaker, and if the Trojans were to repeat as champions, O.J. would have to carry a heavier load, if that can be imagined.

The Trojans opened their 1968 season at Minnesota, and

tension was high as the huge party of players, coaches, press, and alumni flew east. Simpson felt the pressure, too. Although he scored two first-half touchdowns, he also fumbled twice and midway through the fourth quarter, the Gophers led, 20–16.

Pained by a deep bruise in his thigh, Simpson was still the man on whom the Trojans relied in the clutch. With four minutes to play, he was given the ball six straight times. Starting at the Minnesota 45, the Juice cut and slashed, sprinted and bulled downfield for the go-ahead touchdown. And then, in the final seconds, he scored once more.

When the stat crew added up O.J.'s figures, they came to an incredible 39 carries for 236 yards and four touchdowns, plus six pass receptions for 57 more yards. Each of these figures was a career high, and football fans around the world were served notice that Simpson was off and running. He would make his senior season even more spectacular than the year before, if possible. Notice also was served to Heisman Trophy voters and to future Southern Cal opponents.

As the Trojan charter flight returned to Los Angeles, O.J. was met at the airport by his pregnant wife Marguerite. A fan confessed that he had been worried when the Trojans fell behind. "How do you think I felt the second time I fumbled?" O.J. replied. The fumbles were more on his mind than the four touchdowns.

One-sided victories over Northwestern and Miami followed in order. Despite the bruises incurred at Minnesota, O.J. continued to work overtime. In the two games he carried the ball a total of 72 times for five touchdowns.

After three games against intersectional opponents, Southern Cal returned to the Pac-8 family against Stanford, and the Trojans knew that this would be no ordinary game. Coach McKay always took particular delight in needling Stanford, the only other private school in a conference made up mostly of state-supported institutions. McKay liked to refer to Stanford as "Vassar," the East Coast girl's school. In preseason, he would claim that Stanford had the best material in the conference, but that Southern Cal would win the championship. The Trojans had not lost to Stanford since 1957, and their annual meeting had become more than a game in Palo Alto: It was a crusade.

John Ralston, later coach of the Denver Broncos (where he succeeded Lou Saban), had been brought in to rebuild Stanford football. He constantly told his players, "Before you can think of Rose Bowls and championships, you've got to be able to beat Southern Cal." This year he had a pretty good sophomore quarterback to help him do it, Jim Plunkett.

It was a bruised and aching O.J. Simpson who faced these hostile Indians that afternoon in Palo Alto, just down the peninsula from San Francisco. The thigh injury he had suffered in the opener had been aggravated the week before against Miami. The leg was weak and painful, and two assistant coaches, Marv Goux and Craig Fertig, actually had to assist O.J. onto the field for pregame warmups. But slowly the pain began to disappear as he worked it loose and the adrenalin started to flow.

As they had done against Minnesota, the Trojans started slowly against Stanford. With their home crowd of 90,000 fans cheering them on, the Indians began to believe that at last they would achieve a victory over Southern Cal. But they reckoned without the patented O.J. Simpson second half. Like Secretariat running down the field in the stretch, the Juice turned it on in the last two quarters. Shredding the Stanford defense again and again, O.J. scored three touchdowns and gained 220 yards on a school record of 47 carries. The old mark of 45 rushing attempts had been in the books since 1927.

The final score was 27–24, Southern Cal, and Stanford players left the field muttering in awe about O.J. Simpson. "I guess he showed us why he's The Man," tight end Bob Moore declared.

O.J. Simpson, of course, wasn't the only weapon in SC's arsenal. The Trojans also knew how to play defense, and it was this platoon that had to carry the load the next two weeks. Washington fell, 14–7, and the big play was a goal-line stand on the one that was followed by a 99-yard drive to the winning touchdown. The next SC victim was Oregon, 20–13, as O.J. was held to 67 yards on 25 carries.

SC's record now stood at 6 and 0, and it was time to start thinking about conference championships and Rose Bowl invitations. But opponent No. 7, California, had some dreams in this direction, too. The Golden Bears of Berkeley had a 5–1–1 record and the third best defense in the nation. This was a major test for the Trojans, who would then close their season against three extremely tough elevens, Oregon State, UCLA, and Notre Dame. If they failed against Cal, it meant they could write off the rest of the season, because those others would be too tough for them.

Also, out in the Midwest a talented running back who

also played superb defense, Leroy Keyes of Purdue, had established himself as Simpson's major rival for the Heisman Trophy. Heisman ballots soon would be going out to sportswriters around the nation and O.J., despite his strong runnerup finish the year before, was far from an automatic choice. It would behoove him to come up with a big game, quick.

The Cal defense was keyed to stop Simpson, so McKay gambled by going right to the Bears' strength. If you can beat a team at its strong point early, the rest is easy . . . and if you fail you can probe the weaknesses later. So the Trojans gave the ball to O.J. Simpson on the first six plays of the game, and each time he charged right into the middle of the line, right at the heart of Cal's stacked defense. It was no contest. After three quarters Simpson had gained 164 yards on 31 carries and scored two touchdowns. The Trojans were leading, 35–3, at this point and so, for one of the few times in his career, Simpson was given a fourth-quarter vacation. McKay knew his star back had important work ahead the next three weeks.

Next up was Oregon State. The Beavers' record was 7–2, but both losses had been by a single point. None of the Trojans had forgotten that Oregon State had handed them their only defeat the season before. "There's no team we want to beat more," Simpson said solemnly.

You'd have thought Simpson got his scholarship on a piecework basis. So much per run. Almost as if he had to make up for his light day the week before, he carried over and over and over again against the tough Beavers. For the second time that season, his number of carries reached 47, and he gained a career high of 238 yards in the 17–13 victory.

UCLA was next, and this game proved somewhat anti-climactic after the previous year's emotional binge. O.J. carried 40 times for 205 yards, and the 28–16 walkover assured SC of still another Rose Bowl invitation.

But before Pasadena there was the season's finale, Notre Dame in the Los Angeles Coliseum. "This is it," said O.J. "This is why I came to SC, to play in the big time."

The Trojans could package a perfect season and the national championship by winning this game, and the odds looked good for Southern Cal when it was learned that Terry Hanratty, Notre Dame's fine quarterback and another Heisman candidate, would not play because of a knee injury. His place would be taken by a sophomore named Joe Theismann.

Before the game Notre Dame coach Ara Parseghian talked of Simpson in glowing terms.

"He is absolutely fantastic," Parseghian said. "Beyond his 9.3 speed and his 207 pounds, he is the most durable, elusive runner I've ever seen. His stamina is staggering. He is almost guaranteed to carry 40 times against us.

"He never wastes himself, either," Parseghian continued. "If the hole is not there, he will move left or right. It's amazing how he squeezes that 6-2 frame of his through even the smallest piece of daylight.

"He is the most outstanding runner of our time and without doubt the most durable."

However, while praising O.J. Parseghian also was mapping plans to bury him. The Irish scheme consisted of two parts.

The first was basic. O.J. could not run while the Irish had the ball. Notre Dame would have to control it.

This, of course, could not be done indefinitely, so Parseghian and his chief defensive aide, John Ray, devised what they called a "triangle" defense. They felt Simpson was most dangerous when he cut back against the grain, against the defensive flow. So instead of seeking quick penetration, the Irish would surround him. "Containment" was the key word. Ray and Parseghian had been working on this plan for weeks, and in the days before the game, Irish defenders were drilled over and over again on the exercise of patience.

But all these best-laid plans seemed to go up in the smog when young Theismann threw an interception on the second play from scrimmage and Southern Cal's Sandy Durko ran it in for a touchdown and a 7–0 Trojan lead.

It was here that Theismann showed the ingredients of his future stardom. Regaining his poise he directed the Irish on one long scoring drive to tie and another to go ahead. Then, just before the half, he resorted to some trickery. One of the Notre Dame halfbacks, Coley O'Brien, had started his career as a quarterback. Theismann pitched back to O'Brien as if to start a sweep, then he took off downfield and found himself a wide-open receiver when O'Brien stopped short and let the ball fly. This maneuver is legal in college, and the easy touchdown gave Notre Dame a 21–7 halftime lead.

After two quarters O.J.'s stat column showed only nine carries for 23 yards. The Irish had produced 324 yards in total offense to 71 for Southern Cal, and Parseghian's ball control had paid off better than two-to-one, 51 plays to 24 for the home team.

National champions, however, are not made from teams

that give up in the second half. Notre Dame had to kick off to start the third quarter, and Steve Sogge, the Trojans' underrated quarterback, drove his team 65 yards for a touchdown that cut the Irish lead in half. O.J. ran for a seven-yard gain on this drive—his longest sortie of the day—and he capped the advance by bouncing around left end from one yard out for the score.

Finally, in the fourth quarter, Southern Cal struck again, this time on a spectacular 60-yard pass play, Sogge to Sam Dickerson, for a 21–21 tie. And that's the way it ended.

The underdog Irish, of course, were satisfied with the result. They not only had stymied the nation's best team, they had trussed and hog-tied the nation's best runner. Simpson carried the ball 21 times and gained only 55 yards, a career low.

The Rose Bowl would prove even more disappointing. The Trojans had one last shot at the national championship against undefeated Ohio State. But although Simpson ran 80 yards for a touchdown, he also cost his team with late fumbles, and O.J. came up a 27–16 loser in his final college game.

But losing had not exactly been a habit with O.J. Simpson. In two years at Southern Cal the Trojans had compiled a combined record of 19–2–1, including two conference championships, two trips to the Rose Bowl, and a national title. Simpson equaled or broke 13 school records and, in his senior season, he set an NCAA record with 1,709 yards rushing in the regular schedule. You couldn't find an all-America team without his name on it, and wherever they gave away a Player of the Year award, there was O.J. Simpson in his tuxedo to receive it.

All year long Simpson had figured he would be the favorite to win the Heisman Trophy, and he knew he was having the kind of season the voters would appreciate. Only on the eve of the announcement did he begin to experience doubts. But the next morning Dr. Norman Topping, president of Southern Cal, relayed the good news. Simpson felt a distinct feeling of relief as he heard the results making him an overwhelming choice. He piled up 2,853 points to 1,103 for Leroy Keyes and 387 for Hanratty, a distant third. (Electors list three names, in order.) His margin in first-place votes was even more one-sided, 855 to 49 for Keyes and 22 for Hanratty.

At a campus press conference to announce Simpson's award, athletic director Jess Hill disclosed that O.J.'s No. 32 jersey would be retired, the same honor that had been accorded the No. 21 of Mike Garrett.

"O.J. is a great football player, and he has a great and deep sense of humility and appreciation for the other players on the squad and the men on the coaching staff," Hill said.

Then, with the crowd chanting, "O.J., O.J., O.J.," Simpson walked to the microphone.

"I'm proud and happy, and I can't wait to tell the guys on the team," he said. "They contributed as much as I did to winning the Heisman. I take it as a team award."

These sentiments would be recalled five years later almost to the day on the other side of the continent, when O.J. Simpson again would acknowledge his teammates' contribution as he achieved the ultimate as a pro.

6

"Well, It's Not Honolulu"

The Heisman Trophy literally brought O.J. Simpson face to face with cold reality. On an early December day he came to New York for the sponsoring Downtown Athletic Club's formal presentation dinner. The affair was preceded by an afternoon press conference, and as he talked to reporters, O.J.'s glance kept straying toward the window.

No, he wasn't bored by the press conference; he was fascinated by what he saw outside, snow and sleet whipping off New York harbor.

"Does it always snow like this around here?" he asked uncomfortably.

O.J. already had begun to ponder his professional future. The AFL–NFL war had ended with the 1966 merger, and one of the major benefits to the owners was the institution of a combined college draft. The two leagues would remain separate entities for another year, but they already were meeting in a postseason Super Bowl, and they had abandoned their ruinous price war for talent. O.J. would be drafted by one major league pro team in this country, and that's the team for which he would play.

Still a traditionalist who had rooted for the 49ers as a kid and the Rams as a collegian, Simpson hoped that he would be picked by an old-line NFL team. But even more compelling was his desire to play close to home on the West Coast where it was warm. As the 1968 season drew to a close, scouts and press reports were unanimous that O.J. would be the first player drafted, and cities like Philadelphia, Pittsburgh and, ugh, Buffalo were in line for the dubious honor of leading off.

O.J. had heard all the jokes about Buffalo, where supposedly there are only two seasons—the Fourth of July and winter.

"Sure I'd rather play in California than in Buffalo," he told a questioner, and for years he would rue that innocent remark.

He added: "With Buffalo not doing so well, I guess I'm sweating it a little bit more."

Soon after the Rose Bowl concluded his college career, Simpson played in the Hula Bowl. By now Buffalo had assured its position as the worst team in pro football. The Bills' owner, Ralph C. Wilson, Jr., through Los Angeles columnist Mel Durslag, arranged a private interview with Simpson in L.A. soon after the game.

Wilson knew he would be required to make a substantial financial investment in Simpson and that he would be tempted by trade offers from other teams for his lead-off position in the draft. The Rams, for example, had stockpiled three first-round choices through trades and also had enough blue chip veteran personnel to put together an attractive package for his down-and-out club. Wilson had to see what he was getting, if Simpson had the kind of presence to carry a franchise along with his shoulder pads and a football. He also had to start trying to sell Buffalo to the player, and he had to determine if O.J. seemed adaptable enough so that the city's cold and forbidding climate would not prove an insurmountable barrier to enthusiastic performance.

"I've never been to Buffalo, but my image of the town is cars stalled in a blizzard with snow piled to the roofs. Is it really that bad?" Simpson asked in Durslag's account of the conversation.

"Well, it's not Honolulu," Wilson replied, but he pointed out that many Bills' players made the city their year-round home.

They discussed no specifics of money and parted with Wilson offering to fly O.J. and his wife to Buffalo for a visit in February, after the draft. "But maybe we should make it in June," the convivial clubowner joked. He left Simpson with every indication that Buffalo would draft him.

Although Wilson received all sorts of trade offers for the rights to O.J., he never really came close to giving them up. Scouting reports—his own and those from other organizations—agreed unanimously that O.J. Simpson was a rare and gifted football player and easily the best running back of his time.

George Sauer, himself a college football Hall of Famer, was asked that winter by the New York *Daily News* Inquiring Photographer to name the greatest college player he had ever seen. It was expected that he would bring up a storied name from the past, instead he replied without hesitation: "O.J. Simpson." Simpson had only just completed his college career, but Sauer wasn't the type to be blinded by proximity. At that time he was serving as head talent scout for the New York Jets, and his approach to college players had to be completely calculating.

Sauer, whose original scouting report on Joe Namath has become part of pro football's literature, sent in his first comprehensive rating of O.J. early in Simpson's first year at Southern Cal. It is reproduced below. A couple of explanations are necessary. First, the date: November 7, 1967. At this point, O.J. had played barely half a season. The date also is significant in Sauer's comparison of Simpson with Jet halfback Emerson Boozer, who in the first half of his second year as a pro was en route to breaking every scoring record in NFL history. The weekend Sauer filed his report, however, Boozer suffered a horrendous knee injury that kept him from achieving his early promise. The miracle of today is not that Boozer is still an outstanding halfback, but that he is playing at all.

The Jets' rating system as shown on the next-to-bottom line also bears explanation. A "5" in the "pro rating guide" means the scout feels the player "will be a star" in pro ball. A "4" means he will play first-team, "3" that he should be able to make the 40-man squad. A "2" signifies an outside chance of making the squad, and a "1" is a reject. (Years later in the interest of computer conformity with other members of their scouting combo, the Jets reversed the numerical order.)

In his initial report on the young O.J., Sauer rated him

a 4-plus prospect at halfback, a 4 at flanker, and a 4 at cornerback.

Subsequent reports by other scouts would give him near-unanimous fives in all categories, including the sum-up.

As the 1969 draft approached two years later, Sauer ranked all the best halfbacks in the nation for his employers, averaging out the ratings of all his scouts for a final grade. That list also is reproduced here.

Sauer's roster includes some fascinating entries. The distant second prospect behind Simpson is Leroy Keyes, who was placed on defense as a pro, and then there's another big drop to third place, shared by Bobby Douglass, who became a nonpassing pro quarterback in Chicago, and Ron Johnson, now a star with the Giants.

Mercury Morris, Eddie Hinton (who became a receiver), Altie Taylor, Ed Podolak, George Nock, John Fuqua, and Carl Garrett (who beat out Simpson as AFL Rookie of the Year) were other top members of the halfback class of '69.

While pro teams were rating his talents, O.J. also was busy, scouting business agents.

The man he eventually selected was Chuck Barnes, Southern Cal '53, who had earned a good reputation representing automobile race drivers. From a public relations job with the Firestone Corporation, Barnes had formed his own company, Sports Headliners, Inc., out of Indianapolis. His major clients included A.J. Foyt, Parnelli Jones, and Mario Andretti. Later he branched out into other sports and added the Baltimore Colts' Johnny Unitas to his stable.

GOTHAM FOOTBALL CLUB, INC.

595 MADISON AVENUE • NEW YORK, N.Y. 10022 • TELEPHONE: 421-6600

PLAYER'S GRADING FORM

DATE Nov. 7, 1967

☐ SINGLE
☐ MARRIED

AME (Please Print) Simpson (LAST) Orenthal James "O J" (FIRST) (MIDDLE)

U. of Southern Calif. (SCHOOL) Off Halfback (POSITION) 6'1" (HEIGHT) 204 (WEIGHT) 20 (AGE)

San Francisco, Calif. (HOMETOWN) 1965 (INITIAL COLLEGE REGISTRATION) 1967 & (1968) (COMPETITION REMAINING) City College of San Francisco Junior College (IF TRANSFER, LIST PREVIOUS SCHOOL)

PEED IF TIMED: ____ yards in ____ Sec. (IN FOOTBALL TOGS) 100 yards 9.4 Sec. (IN SHORTS)

RATING SCALE: 5 Outstanding 4 Above Average 3 Average 2 Below Average 1 Poor

USING ABOVE RATING SCALE, GRADE PLAYER ON EACH OF FOLLOWING CHARACTERISTICS:

1. QUICKNESS	5 – 4 – 3 – 2 – 1	6. SIZE POTENTIAL	5 – 4 – 3 – 2 – 1
2. AGILITY	5 – 4 – 3 – 2 – 1	7. SPEED FOR POSITION	5 – 4 – 3 – 2 – 1
3. STRENGTH	5 – 4 – 3 – 2 – 1	8. CHARACTER	5 – 4 – 3 – 2 – 1
4. TOUGHNESS	5 – 4 – 3 – 2 – 1	9. AGGRESSIVENESS	5 – 4 – 3 – 2 – 1
5. DESIRE	5 – 4 – 3 – 2 – 1	10. PRIDE	5 – 4 – 3 – 2 – 1

SE POSITION GUIDE ON REVERSE SIDE & COMMENT ON ITEMS LISTED FOR HIS POSITION:

FFENSIVE ABILITY: "This man is a fast Emerson Boozer". He has exceptional quickness, speed, balance and toughness - also POISE ! Coach John McKay says he could also be an outstanding Cornerback. He was an All-American Junior College Defensive Back! He has great reaction,

EFENSIVE ABILITY: range and is a very sure tackler ! An Outstanding Prospect in this, his Junior year ! Is also a fine receiver ! His legs, below the knees, are not big, nor does he look like he weighs 204, but it's "all there" !

F A SPECIALIST, EVALUATE HIS ABILITY: ____

EST POSITION FOR PRO FOOTBALL, AND WHY? Off. Halfback Flanker Cornerback

SING THE PRO RATING GUIDE (5 – 4 – 3 – 2 – 1) I RATE HIM 4+ 4 (ON OFFENSE) AND 4 (ON DEFENSE)
(Shown on Reverse Side)

COUT: Sauer TEAM: ____

1969 Common Draft

Offensive Halfbacks

Grade	Name	School	Ht.	Wt.	"40" Speed	Remarks
4.6	Simpson, O. J.	U. Southern California	6′1″	207	4.3	The greatest!
4.2	Keyes, Leroy	Purdue University	6′3″	205	4.5	Great Prospect. Does much by instinct
3.8	Douglass, Robert	Univ. of Kansas	6′3″	215	4.8	Strong arm & runner
3.8	Johnson, Ronald	Univ. of Michigan	6′1″	196	4.7	Fine runner, good hands. Fair blocker
3.7	Morris, Eugene	West Texas State Univ.	5′10″	190	4.5	Great runner. Very shifty & tough. Fine hands. Fine returner!
3.6	Brown, Terry	Oklahoma State Univ.	6′2″	208	4.6	Quick & tough. Good prospect
3.6	Campbell, Bob	Penn State Univ.	5′11″	185	4.6	Quick, tough, fine Player!
3.6	Hinton, Eddie	Univ. of Oklahoma	6′1″	200	4.6	Fine hands & speed. Question toughness
3.6	Irby, George	Tuskegee Institute	6′4″	220	4.6	Fine hands & speed, tough, strong. May be a TE
3.6	Lyons, Dick	Univ. of Kentucky	5′11″	188	4.7	Tough, emotional, quick, balance. Fine hands. Is very OK!
3.6	Taylor, Altie	Utah State Univ.	5′11″	195	4.6	Strong, quick & tough. Good blocker
3.5	Gilbert, Chris	Univ. of Texas	5′10″	180	4.7	Great competitor. Great quickness & balance
3.5	Gipson, Paul	Univ. of Houston	6′½″	208	4.7	Fine running ability. Is OK
3.5	Gladieux, Robert	Univ. of Notre Dame	5′11″	188	4.65	Fine competitor, good speed. Tough
3.5	Nock, George	Morgan State College	5′10½″	198	4.65	Fine balance, fast & shifty. Lacks size.
3.5	Podolak, Edward	Univ. of Iowa	6′1″	192	4.75	Fine competitor. Good runner. Quick Could be OK
3.4	Blackney, Harry	Univ. of Maryland	6′1″	225	4.8	Tough! Is OK!
3.4	Fuqua, John	Morgan State College	5′11″	197	4.7	Quick, tough, shifty
3.4	Garrett, Carl	New Mexico Highlands U.	5′10″	200	4.6	Quick, strong, & shifty
3.4	Grate, Willie	South Carolina State Col.	6′4″	220	4.6	Fine speed. Not good blocker. Needs experience
3.4	Moore, Dickie	Western Kentucky Univ.	6′0″	202	4.65	Very fine runner. Hurt much
3.4	Pappas, Nick	Memphis State Univ.	5′11″	190	4.65	Explosive runner. Good hands & tough

Barnes first met Simpson on a visit to the Southern Cal locker room in 1967, at which time O.J. introduced the short but dapper business agent to Earl McCullouch. Barnes eventually handled McCullouch's signing with the Detroit Lions, and Simpson was impressed with the contract that he obtained for Earl the Pearl. As his senior season drew to a close, Simpson was besieged by hordes of instant friends offering advice for a fee. He asked Barnes to help him pick an agent, but then they both decided it was silly to go to a third party. Their friendship and business relationship continues, and Barnes has moved his Sports Headliners office to Los Angeles.

The NFL draft is held under unique circumstances. Because their scouting procedures are so computerized, the coaches and general managers usually operate out of their respective home offices, hooked up by telephone to the drafting headquarters in a New York hotel. Each team has an agent on the other end of the phone, but usually it's a publicity man, minor team functionary, or friend of the coach. Kansas City sends its trainer.

Buffalo's man in the spotlight was Lou Sahadi, a sports magazine editor who suddenly found himself in position to make a little news of his own. Lou lives in New Jersey, and his night before the draft was a sleepless one, interspersed with nightmares that saw him fail to wake in time, thus costing the Bills their precious lead-off pick.

The draft was scheduled to start at 10 in the morning, New York time, but half an hour earlier—6:30 A.M. in California—O.J. was awakened from a deep sleep at his mother-in-law's house in San Francisco. Ralph Wilson was calling to confirm what he had told O.J. the night before. No NFL team had come up with an offer that he couldn't refuse, and so the Buffalo Bills were making Simpson their first pick. (O.J. was less surprised at this news than by the fact that the Bills had been able to track him down at his in-law's.)

"I'm very happy we're taking you," Wilson said.

"I'm happy, too," the Juice replied, somewhat less enthusiastically.

Then John Rauch, Buffalo's new coach who had first seen Simpson play at City College of San Francisco when he was coaching the Oakland Raiders, got on the phone. "I hope we can get together soon and start talking football. We've got a lot of work to do," Rauch said eagerly.

It would be many months before they were able to do that.

The first salary discussions between Wilson and Barnes took place in Detroit in early March. Barnes seemed obsessed with the contract obtained by running back Donny Anderson from Green Bay in 1966 for a reputed $600,000. "We think O.J. is worth more than Anderson," Barnes declared.

Wilson agreed, with one major demurrer. Anderson, he pointed out, had been able to capitalize on the pro football war. The Packers had been forced to outbid Houston of the AFL for his services. Simpson did not have this competitive luxury.

"What players got during the war is irrelevant and doesn't pertain to today's circumstances," Wilson said. "The clubs stopped the war for only one reason, to avoid going bankrupt."

Later in the negotiations Barnes added another item to

the package. He wanted a $500,000 loan that O.J. could use for investment purposes. The term of the contract and loan would be five years.

"What am I, a banker?" Wilson asked Mel Durslag, his columnist confidant who also may have been polishing his one-liners. "Why I don't even own a pinstripe suit. I'm not sure even Howard Hughes can handle this kind of package."

Wilson called Barnes' opening gambit "depressing" and said he had a good counteroffer in mind. The Bills' annual budget for player salaries was $1 million. He would give O.J. the whole million and then let Simpson pay his teammates.

Barnes and Simpson were not amused. The wisecracks were funny, but there had been an agreement to keep silent about the negotiations, and they felt Wilson's comments were a breach of faith. Simpson, even then mindful of his image, was incensed that Wilson would try to color him greedy.

Barnes later dropped the loan issue temporarily but raised his asking price on the contract to $650,000, including a $150,000 bonus for signing. He pointed out that Simpson's presence in the lineup would have a direct bearing on the Bills' income. They would sell more tickets since their park was not an automatic sellout, and their exhibition schedule, a major source of revenue, already had been upgraded. The year before they had played preseason games in Rochester, Cincinnati, and Tulsa. This summer they had been booked into Houston's Astrodome, Detroit, the Los Angeles Coliseum, and Cleveland as part of Art Modell's popular doubleheader extravaganza. The change was striking and some of the contracts reportedly contained penalties for O.J.'s nonappearance.

Wilson, meanwhile, offered Simpson a flat $50,000 per year for five years, which put him and Barnes a mere $400,000 apart.

The impasse continued through the spring as both sides mulled their options.

Because the AFL–NFL merger had not been fully implemented at this point, Wilson could offer Simpson's rights in trade only to the nine other AFL teams. He said he made inquiries in this direction but only to the handful of strong teams that had enough talent to give him the players O.J. was worth. None of these, Wilson reported, was willing to deal for an unsigned Simpson.

Simpson, for his part, could sit out a year waiting for the full merger when Wilson would have 25 teams with which to deal, or he could sue to overturn the draft structure. This could take years during which his football skills would disappear. Worse, during either hiatus his value as a commercial property also would deteriorate.

The Canadian League was never a strong factor, but for a while a couple of minor leagues stirred up some headlines. The San Antonio Toros of the Texas League said they would promise Simpson 80 percent of their net gate from eight home games against a flat fee of $15,000 for each of 16 league games, or $240,000 for the year. The Indianapolis Capitols of the Continental League—representing, surprise, Barnes' home town—offered a $400,000 package. Of this $150,000 would be salary, the rest a loan.

Still another Continental League team, the Orlando Panthers, made a very intriguing pitch. The Florida eleven asked the state citrus commission to help underwrite a $600,000 Simpson contract in order to use his famous initials to promote their leading product. (The circumstances must have made Simpson recall how Southern Cal Athletic Director Jess Hill once had killed a publicity photo of O.J. drinking a glass of orange juice because it might subsequently be used commercially. Hill did not want the Juice exploited and told Simpson, "You're here to play football, not sell orange juice.")

The citrus commission, however, nixed the deal. It had just renewed its promotional contract with singer Anita Bryant, and there was no money left over. The world's greatest halfback was aced out by a soprano.

The minor league deals would have been for one year only, with no option clause, enabling Simpson to try again in the NFL after the full merger. But, in truth . . . as he admitted later . . . there was no way O.J. Simpson would have agreed to play anywhere but in the NFL. It would be like hiring Picasso to paint an outhouse, Heifitz to play a high school square dance.

The whole charade may have been put in proper context when the Indianapolis Capitols put out a national press release more than two legal-sized pages long just to announce its *withdrawal* from the O.J. sweepstakes.

During the late spring and summer when he was not busy making no progress with Wilson, Barnes wasn't exactly idle. Simpson had come out of college as one of the most popular and highly visible players in the history of college football. His decision to play at Southern Cal was paying off with more than trophies to put in the den of his new $100,000-plus Bel Air home high above the Los Angeles smog belt. (He also bought his mother a home in San Francisco.)

Some felt sorry for O.J. because he had come along too late to capitalize on the pro football war, but O.J. was not unhappy. He knew he was just in time for a different "war," the black revolution. Black had become commercial as well as beautiful. There were black movies, companies sent out the call for black executives, and for the first time black athletes would be able to cash in richly on endorsements. Before long Simpson would claim that he ranked second only to Joe Namath in off-field income.

Barnes exploited Simpson's popularity but with caution. He avoided schlock movie productions and get-it-quick business proposals. Instead he hooked Simpson up with reputable companies under long-term programs that would insure his future. One of these was with the American Broadcasting Company, which would more or less sponsor Simpson's budding television career. His pay would depend on his availability, and the first year this connection was worth a reported $35,000.

The two industrial accounts lined up by Barnes must have struck Simpson with irony as he considered how far he had come over the years. One was with the Chevrolet division of General Motors. Under the three-year arrangement, Simpson was in position to make $250,000. Not bad for a kid who used to have to steal the company's product to go for a ride. The other account was with Royal Crown Cola for a minimum of $120,000 over three years and marked the second time O.J. had been employed by this particular soft drink company.

The previous occasion had been the first summer he

was enrolled at Southern Cal. The athletic department got him a job driving an R.C. truck. O.J. recalls it as torturous work under the blazing Los Angeles sun. Unloading the full cases, his wrists would be scratched raw by the bottle caps. Loading empties was worse. Nobody ever completely drains a soft drink bottle, and when he lifted the crates up on the truck, the sticky residue dripped on his head and down his arms. The flies loved it, but O.J. was less than enamored of his job, and his performance reflected this. R.C. fired him after three days. For his efforts on the truck he had been paid $3.25 an hour. The new deal was slightly more lucrative . . . and easier work.

Simpson's patience began to wear short after a face-to-face meeting with Wilson in May, when he demanded again to be traded and stormed angrily out of the club-owner's office.

By now, time was becoming a factor. Simpson had to pass up both major all-star games sponsored by the coach's association and the Chicago *Tribune.* He especially felt bad about missing the prestigious Chicago affair against the world champion Jets and Joe Namath. But both sets of all-star promoters were unable to meet his understandable demand for $500,000 insurance against a disabling injury rather than the standard $25,000. (Once he signed, the Bills would have been liable for his contract if he was hurt in these authorized games.)

In mid-July, the Bills reported to their Niagara University training camp, but Simpson was busy running around the country fulfilling his business commitments, and Barnes was still deadlocked with Wilson.

The Bills opened their preseason schedule against the

Houston Oilers August 2 and were defeated, 24–7, but by now O.J. Simpson was getting itchy. He had been watching his friends on the Los Angeles Rams getting ready for their exhibition opener, and he longed to get to work himself. The Bills had sent him a jersey to wear for a magazine cover photo and occasionally he would put it on and pose wistfully before the mirror. He knew he would not be happy sitting out a year, and Barnes knew his business angels also would be displeased because they thought they had hired a football player to represent them.

The next week the Bills beat the Washington Redskins in Buffalo, 21–17, and the day after the game Simpson agreed to terms.

A key figure in the resolution was Don Augustine, a San Diego attorney who had once represented the AFL Players Association. Wilson knew him from this connection and accepted Augustine's offer to try to make a deal with Barnes. Wilson thought Barnes might appreciate Augustine's professional expertise in this area. A meeting was set up that Saturday morning in Augustine's office in San Diego. The attorney shut the door and said he didn't want anyone to leave until a contract had been settled. Barnes and Simpson were anxious to sign, too. By 5 in the afternoon, after much phoning back and forth with Wilson, they reached agreement. Simpson called Rauch, who was viewing films of the victory over Washington, and said he'd report on Tuesday. At first Rauch thought the call was a practical joke.

Final terms of the four-year contract called for an initial salary of $50,000 with built-in raises and incentive bonuses based on performance and things like all-star and rookie awards. With Barnes coming down considerably in his salary demands, Wilson agreed to provide a $100,000 loan for a total four-year package well in excess of $300,000. There also was an annuity involved, and Wilson said O.J.'s contract was the most lucrative for any player coming out of college since the merger.

Adding up all the deals he had made for his client, Barnes boasted that "over the next four-year period, O.J. Simpson has a guaranteed income of $950,000."

Not bad for the kid from Potrero Hill, but now he had to earn it.

"I had a dream just before the draft. It was a nightmare. I dreamed I was drafted by the Buffalo Bills," Simpson had joked to Wilson one day early in the negotiations.

"That's nothing, I had a nightmare, too," Wilson replied. "I also dreamed we drafted you . . . and you were a flop."

7

Once They Were Champions

Unless the team that selects him has obtained its lead-off position through a trade, pro football's No. 1 draft choice inevitably faces a traumatic experience when he turns professional. To rate as No. 1 pro prospect in the nation, the young man has had to prove he's a winner. He has played most of his career on winning teams. However, the club he is joining is bound to be awful. The team with the worst record in pro football always achieves that distincton on merit.

The Buffalo Bills, when O.J. Simpson joined them, were just such a team. But they also represented a franchise with a tradition. Once, and not so long ago, they had been champions. But, as Simpson was to discover, this created an even more difficult situation, because many of the holdovers from those championship years were still around, creating a bitter cleavage on the squad. The best kind of team, in any sport, combines experience and youth. This holds true if it represents a gradual blend. With the Bills there was no middle ground. The youth consisted of rookies barely starting to shave; the experience quotient was provided by too many veterans on, literally, their last leg.

Still, there was the benefit of a strong pro football tradition in Buffalo, dating all the way back to the 1920s, when the city was represented in various prehistoric leagues.

Following these failures there was a hiatus of almost 20 years until 1946, when the ill-fated All-America Conference was founded as a rival to the National Football League.

The idea of an AAC first surfaced in 1944, at which time the various franchises began to set up their organizations to prepare for the day when the troops would start marching home from World War II.

The honor of being the first of these went to Buffalo. Jim Bruiel, owner of the Frontier Fuel Oil Company, who had been involved in some of that city's earlier pro efforts, was the owner. He hired Lowell "Red" Dawson to be his coach.

However, the most farsighted of the AAC's charter members was in Cleveland, where a taxicab tycoon named Mickey McBride hired a naval officer named Paul Brown to run his team. (It was through McBride that the term taxi squad entered pro football's lexicon. He put Brown's extra players to work driving his cabs so that they'd be available when needed.) Brown, after whom the team was named, was a football genius who left nothing to chance. He even paid Otto Graham a $250 monthly retainer while the former Northwestern star was in service so that he'd sign with the new league upon his discharge.

Founders of the AAC originally had been rebuffed when they sought franchies in the established NFL, a pattern that would be repeated more than a decade later. When reporters asked him to comment about the new league that was getting ready to go into business, NFL Commissioner Elmer Layden snorted, "First, let 'em get a football."

(Almost 20 years later NFL Commissioner Pete Rozelle recalled his predecessor's remark when asked about competition from a proposed World Football League. Taking note that the WFL's organizers were the same men who had formed the American Basketball Association that became famous for its multihued ball, Rozelle told a press conference, "Well, they haven't contacted me, and all I know is what I've read about them in the papers. But, to paraphrase Elmer Layden, let them get themselves a red, white, and blue football." Rozelle quickly added that he was only making a little joke. He didn't want his wisecrack to come back to haunt him the way Layden's had. The brief war with the AAC cost NFL owners millions of dollars.)

The AAC was a strong, well-supported football league. It had good players in generally strong cities with capable ownership and direction. What it lacked was a team that could challenge the Cleveland Browns and a television contract. The Browns won every one of the league's four championships. Only after they moved over to the NFL and proved just as successful did this posthumously repair the reputation of their AAC opposition. More critical was the absence of TV money to provide a financial cushion. The new league was 10 years ahead of its time. Most of its stronger entries matched the NFL in gate attendance, but it did not have the cash to fight a continuing dollar battle for players.

The Buffalo Bills—known as Bisons their first year—had a bona fide star in quarterback George Ratterman, and after the young Notre Dame product joined them their second year, they averaged over 31,000 fans. In 1948 their Chet Mutryn led the AAC in scoring with 16 touchdowns, and the Bills beat Baltimore in a playoff for the Eastern Division championship. This was a dubious honor, carrying with it the privilege of being destroyed by the Browns in the title game, 49–7.

Unfortunately, there were not enough Browns and Bills in the AAC. After four years of red ink that cost the combined teams a reported $4 million (pocket change compared to what the next war would cost), the new league sued for peace. The treaty was signed on NFL terms with only three AAC teams, Cleveland, San Francisco and Baltimore (which folded in a year), being absorbed into the established circuit.

Buffalo fans were stunned at the snub. A petition containing 25,000 pledges to buy season tickets was forwarded to the NFL office. A local stock drive raised $177,600 in 24 hours. But Bert Bell, commissioner of the NFL, was adamant. Business conditions were poor in Buffalo, he said, and he didn't care much for the city's weather. Buffalo was out in the cold and would stay out. Tough bananas.

Ten years exactly after the AAC's final season, the scenario was to be written again. In that decade pro football's popularity soared to undreamed-of heights . . . and television money became a substantial black-ink figure in every budget. Dozens of individuals and syndicates fought to obtain franchises, but all were turned down.

One of these was a 26-year-old Texas millionaire named Lamar Hunt whose diffident manner concealed a will of iron. Hunt had hoped to buy the struggling Chicago Cardinals and move the club to Dallas. Stymied here, Hunt decided to form his own league, and he sought out others who had been similarly disappointed. The first man he contacted was another young Texas oil millionaire whom he had never met, Bud Adams of Houston. Adams also had sought to buy the Cardinals. He thought the idea of a rival American Football League was just dandy, and he put in with Hunt.

Soon the Texans had four other partners, and so they called a press conference to announce their existence and their intention to go into business the following season—1960. The announcement received widespread publicity, which was a good thing. The story even reached the little upstate New York town of Saratoga where a Detroit millionaire named Ralph C. Wilson, Jr., had gone for the August thoroughbred racing season. Wilson, another young sportsman whose money came from trucking and insurance, also had dreams of owning his own team. But the best he could do was a very small piece of the Detroit Lions. Wilson quickly got in touch with Hunt, and they set up a meeting.

Wilson's first thought was to put a franchise in Miami, where he had a home, but the University of Miami, correctly fearing what competition from the pros would do to its own football program, refused to loosen its hold on the Orange Bowl. The city fathers, recalling the Miami Seahawks, which had been forced to drop out of the AAC after one season of meterological disaster, didn't press the issue. For the second straight time, pro football in Miami had been done in by a Hurricane, this one with a capital H. Shut out of the city's only suitable stadium, Wilson left.

He was discouraged, but Hunt and others suggested that he explore other cities, including Buffalo. Wilson did not like the idea of owning a team in a city where he had no roots. He feared the carpet-bagger image. But, hearing good things about the town's football history, he agreed to visit Buffalo.

Here the arm of coincidence reached in. Wilson had served with distinction on a Navy minesweeper during World War II, and his commanding officer was George Schaaf, a Buffalo building contractor. Wilson looked him up when he got to Buffalo, and Schaaf regaled him with stories of how well the fans had supported their old Bills and how disappointed they had been at losing out in the merger. These stories confirmed what Wilson had heard from Detroit sportswriters. He later talked with Paul Neville, managing editor of the Buffalo *Courier-Express*, who assured Wilson his team would receive major league coverage. The mayor and council members promised to enlarge War Memorial Stadium, and so that day, with a handshake, Ralph Wilson agreed to put an AFL team in Buffalo.

Thus, on October 17, 1959, Buffalo became a charter member of the AFL, and before the year was out Wilson had named his team the Bills, drafted Penn State's Richie Lucas to play quarterback, hired Lions' assistant Buster

Ramsey to be his head coach, and—in one of his most astute moves—named former Paul Brown associate Dick Gallagher as general manager.

The Buffalo Bills were in business.

Ramsey was acknowledged as a strong defensive coach, but there were many who felt he could take a team only so far. Eventually, after two straight losing seasons, Wilson came to agree. He fired Ramsey and replaced him with Lou Saban, who had been brought in that year to run the Bills' player personnel department after being fired as head coach at midseason by the Boston Patriots.

Saban, powerfully built, intense, had been a linebacker and defensive captain with the old Cleveland Browns. He brought a hard-nosed dedication to his task. Some of his old players in Boston had called him ruthless. In later years they would go all out to beat him, succeeding often even when the Bills had more talent. Saban was constantly on the lookout to improve his team, even on the fly during the season. He would not keep a player around simply because the man might upgrade his team by one or two victories in the standings. He wanted only players whom he could envision as being champions. Once he made a negative judgment, the player was as good as gone.

(In contrast, the man who succeeded Saban in Boston, Mike Holovak, had success with a different formula. He felt that continuity was an important ingredient in winning. Once he picked his squad in training camp, he would make no changes unless forced by injury or by a complete breakdown in performance. He won, too, for awhile until his owner's penuriousness made it impossible for the Patriots to compete for talent.)

The Bills had a pretty fair nucleus when Saban took over—one reason Ramsey had been fired for not doing more with them—and three prizes were rookie offensive linemen Billy Shaw, Al Bemiller, and Stew Barber. They would anchor the offense for years to come. Saban's own heart was in the defense, and over the years he brought in some superstuds for this department like Tom Sestak, Jim Dunaway, Mike Stratton, George Saimes, and Butch Byrd.

Saban, a physical man, preferred this approach for his teams. They didn't finesse, they mauled opponents. He had a preference for the run, and he finally found his man for the 1962 season in Carlton C. (Cookie) Gilchrist. Gilchrist was a legend in his own time up in Canada, and American players would come back from the northland absolutely awestruck by his Bunyanesque feats as he played both offense and defense.

Gilchrist had tried out with the Cleveland Browns right out of high school and almost made it. When he failed he went to play in Canada.

Gilchrist's problem was that he believed in what might euphemistically be called "creative accounting." It's said that he used one advance from a football team that was supposed to set him up in an off-season business to carpet his house. In later years he pointed out that he had earned over $300,000 from pro football. "I'm just like J. Paul Getty," he joked. "We've both earned a lot of money, only he got into the habit of saving it, and I got into the habit of spending it."

Gilchrist used to advise young players to seek salary advances from their teams. "Always stay as far ahead as you can, that way it's more difficult for them to trade you," he chuckled.

It didn't always work out that way, however. His financial scrapes and temperament kept him moving from one Canadian club to another, and when he ran out of teams Saban corraled him for the Bills. After paying off more than $5,000 he had owed his last employer, of course.

Gilchrist became an instant running star with the Bills, gaining more than 900 yards each of the three seasons he lasted with them. In 1962, his American debut, he became the first AFL runner to rush for over 1,000 yards. The memory of Gilchrist's success under Saban eventually would have a major influence on O.J. Simpson's career in Buffalo.

Even with Gilchrist the Bills started the 1962 season slowly, to say the least, with five straight losses. Most of these were at home, and the natives were plainly restless. After one defeat they showered Saban and his players with beer cans as they left the field. Buffalo is a blue-collar city, a beer-and-a-shot sort of place. To show how angry and frustrated those Buffalo fans were, most of the beer cans they rifled at the Bills weren't even empty.

Just in time, though, the Bills found the magic formula with a new quarterback and began to win. They lost only one of their last nine and ended up with their first winning record in history, 7–6–1.

Saban often was referred to as a "garbage man" who loved to cull the waiver lists for other team's rejects in a constant campaign to upgrade his team. And Saban didn't mind the title, either, even though it kept his players (like those in Boston) in a constant state of apprehension. During the 1962 season he pulled off one of his greatest coups.

There had been an unwritten understanding in the AFL that players put on emergency injured waivers just before a game would not be claimed. Sid Gillman, general manager and coach of the San Diego Chargers, was counting on this when he sent the name of quarterback Jack Kemp into the league office the day before a game in Houston. Kemp was suffering from a dislocated finger that needed several weeks' rest. The Chargers' other quarterbacks were hurt, too, and so Gillman had to make room on his roster. When Saban saw Kemp's name on the waiver wire, his eyes lit up like a pinball machine. Kemp was an established star, and the Bills' crying need ever since their inception had been for a quality quarterback. Saban put in a claim for Kemp, whose name could no longer be withdrawn because Gillman, in his haste, already had filled the roster spot. Jack Kemp became a Bill for $100. It was the biggest bargain in pro football since the Baltimore Colts got Johnny Unitas for a phone call. In San Diego Gillman was livid, but there was nothing he could do. The written rules offered no recourse. (Just to show that Saban wasn't the worst guy in the league, two other teams also had claimed Kemp, but Buffalo got first dibs because of its 0–3 record.)

With Kemp healthy all the next year, the Bills repeated their 7–6–1 record in 1963, and this mark turned out to be good enough to tie Boston for the Eastern Division championship. The two teams met in Fenway Park after the game was delayed more than an hour so the field could be cleared of snow, and Boston's jinx over Saban continued. The Patriots won, 26–8, but then went out to San Diego for the AFL title game to be slaughtered by the Chargers, 51–10. Even without Kemp, whom Gillman later privately intimated was unable to win the big ones, the Chargers were one helluva team.

A year later, however, the Bills were ready. They won their first nine and even survived a late-season revolt by Cookie Gilchrist to win the East with a 12–2 record. That earned them the right to play host to the Chargers for the league crown. Even without ace receiver Lance Alworth, who was injured, the Chargers were a formidable lot. They swept to a quick 7–0 lead and were driving for another TD when fullback Keith Lincoln took a short swing pass from Tobin Rote and then was leveled by Mike Stratton's devastating tackle. It was one of the most punishing tackles ever seen on national television—or anywhere else, for that matter. Lincoln was prostrate, writhing in pain, and finally had to be helped off the field with broken ribs. The play—a clean shot—took all the starch out of the Chargers. The Bills could sense it and rolled to a 20–7 victory.

The next year, after Gilchrist had been shipped off in a trade to Denver, the Bills went 10–3–1 in regular season for another Eastern title. Again they were to play the Chargers and this time San Diego, as home team, was favored. But even though star Buffalo guard Billy Shaw was knocked out on one of the first plays and had to miss the whole first half, the Bills won even more decisively, 23–0. "We is established," Jack Kemp exulted in the afterglow of a second straight "big game" victory over the team that had let him go.

Lou Saban, honored for the second straight time as Coach of the Year, said simply and characteristically, "We whipped them in the trenches."

UPI TELEPHOTO

O.J. Simpson runs 13 yards through a forest of UCLA tacklers for Southern Cal's second touchdown in a 21–20 victory that clinched a Rose Bowl invitation in O.J.'s first year with the Trojans.

UPI TELEPHOTO

The power and intensity that make an O.J. Simpson are evident as he takes this handoff in a Southern Cal workout.

UPI TELEPHOTO

Once he ran track, too. O.J. takes the baton from teammate Fred Kuller in 440-yard relay in Pacific-Eight Conference championships his senior year. Earlier O.J. had helped SC set a world record in that event.

UPI PHOTO

O.J. Simpson and Southern Cal coach John McKay.

O.J. closes in on goal line against California his senior year.

O.J. greets injured Terry Hanratty after Southern Cal and Notre Dame battled to 21–21 tie.

BOTH PHOTOS:
UPI TELEPHOTO

UPI TELEPHOTOS

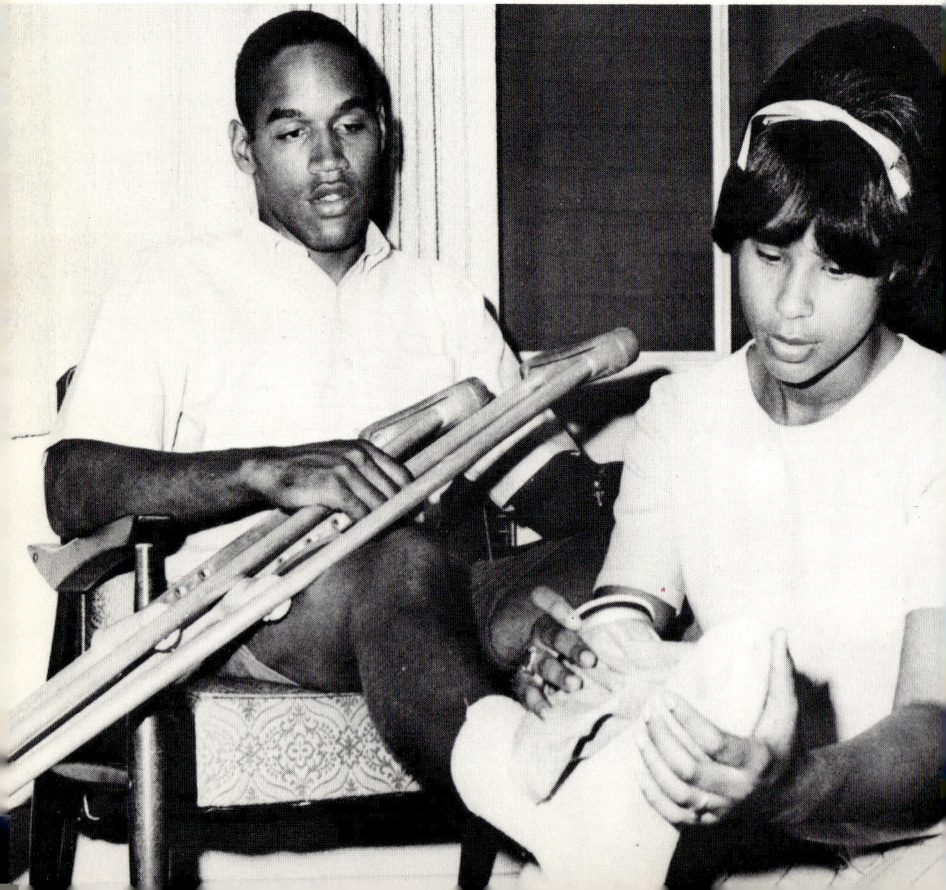

DOWNTOWN AC PHOTO BY ARTHUR J. GORR

ABOVE: *O.J. in tux, receiving the Heisman Trophy at a formal dinner at the Downtown Athletic Club in New York.*

OPPOSITE PAGE: *Margeurite Simpson shares the glory and the pain with O.J. Above, they're on the platform for the announcement that O.J. has just won the Heisman Trophy. Below, during his junior year, Margeurite applies an ice pack to O.J.'s injured ankle.*

UPI TELEPHOTO

ABOVE: *O.J. Simpson nuzzles a toy buffalo and tries to look happy after learning that the Bills have just drafted him.*

UPI TELEPHOTO

UPI TELEPHOTO

Bare-headed because there's no helmet to fit him and wearing an unfamiliar No. 36 jersey, O.J. Simpson engages in his first workout with the Bills.

LEFT: *The city of Buffalo turns out to greet O.J. at the airport after he finally signs his contract. That's Miss Buffalo, Kathleen Karpinski, wearing the crown and Mayor Frank Sedita at right.*

UPI TELEPHOTO

Teammates Joe O'Donnell (left) and Al Cowlings, his boyhood friend, carry O.J. off the field after Simpson has hurt his knee against the Bengals.

UPI TELEPHOTO

Playing the fame game. Top, Miami coach Don Shula adjusts O.J. Simpson's boutonniere before they are honored by New York Chapter of Pro Football Writers of America after 1972 season along with Washington Redskins' Larry Brown (left) and New York Giant president Wellington Mara. Below, it's one of the million award luncheons with the ever-present press conference, this one as Life Saver of the Month.

UPI TELEPHOTO

O.J. Simpson brandishes game ball after he sets NFL record by gaining 250 yards against the New England Patriots in first game of 1973 season.

Weeb Ewbank, long an admirer of O.J. Simpson, makes it a point to show up and congratulate the Buffalo running star after he's received the Hickok Pro Athlete of the Year award from company president John Cosby (right).

UPI TELEPHOTO

O.J. shows he can, indeed, run on snow as he gains some of his 219 yards against the Patriots in next-to-last game of record 1973 campaign. That's New England linebacker Ron Acks (51) on his back.

BOTH PHOTOS: N.Y. DAILY NEWS PHOTO

ABOVE: *O.J. Simpson escapes grasp of New York Jets Mark Lomas (84) on the run that enabled him to break Jim Brown's 10-year-old NFL single-season record.*

LEFT: *Referee Bob Frederic hands O.J. Simpson the ball after he's broken Jim Brown's single season record at New York's Shea Stadium. Later in game he was to get another ball when he went over 2,000 yards.*

N.Y. DAILY NEWS PHOTO

O.J. Simpson brought all his teammates into the press conference after he capped his 2,000-yard season against the Jets. Below, his satisfaction and happiness shine through as he answers questions.

UPI TELEPHOTO

N.Y. DAILY NEWS PHOTO

This is what it's all about. Overjoyed teammates carry exultant O.J. Simpson to the sidelines after he's just become the first NFL running back in history to gain over 2,000 yards in a single season.

This moment would be the high point of the Bills' history. Exactly one week later Saban shocked the football world by announcing his resignation to return to college coaching with the University of Maryland. There were several reasons. He was tired of the bitter war for talent with the NFL. He had neither forgotten nor forgiven Buffalo fans for their beer can barrage in 1962. And he wanted a long-term contract plus, possibly, the general manager's job, too.

Saban had been operating under a handshake agreement with the stunned Wilson, who later would say, "Lou could have had the job as long as he wanted . . . and he knew it because I told him so."

The Buffalo team Saban left behind wasn't quite a hollow shell, but there were cracks in the structure. The team was aging—remember, many of Saban's "new faces" had put in time with other clubs—and the 1965 draft, Saban's last, would be the first of three straight total disasters. Joe Collier, a popular member of Saban's staff, was named the new head coach.

The Bills had enough left to win their third straight Eastern title in 1966 by winning their last game of the season. But then they lost in the championship game to Kansas City by a one-sided 31–7, and thus forfeited their chance to play in the first Super Bowl after the merger.

Following this season the Bills let themselves be talked into a trade that ranks at the opposite end of the spectrum from their steal of Kemp. They traded Daryle Lamonica, their fifth-year second-string quarterback, and a forgettable end named Glenn Bass to the Oakland Raiders for Tom Flores, an experienced quarterback who had just enjoyed his finest season, and wide receiver Art Powell, one of the AFL's all-time greats. Draft choices also were involved. With an older quarterback in Kemp, it was hard to see what the Bills wanted in Flores, although he could conceivably challenge for the top job and provide experienced depth if he didn't beat out the incumbent. Powell figured to be a major plus.

The key man for Oakland was Lamonica, whom Raider boss Al Davis figured was just ready to explode into stardom. How right he was. Lamonica took over as the No. 1 quarterback and directed Oakland right into the Super Bowl.

As for Buffalo the trade was a wipeout. Flores, bedeviled by a series of injuries, failed to throw a single touchdown pass in his two years with the Bills. Powell turned out to be finished. He played only one season during which he caught 20 balls, and that was it. The Bills plummeted to a 4–10 record. The proud Wilson, who had only reluctantly agreed to the trade, was mortified, especially when his fellow owners started to tease him about having been slickered.

Collier's first real name was Joel. But when he became head coach, and a name in the news, so many reporters got it wrong and referred to him as just plain Joe that he finally dropped the final letter. In more ways than one, Collier got the "l" kicked out of him as a head coach.

Entering his third season Collier knew he was in trouble. After being embarrassed by a 37–7 exhibition game loss to Houston two weeks before the opener, he panicked. The next day he called for an all-out scrimmage. Normally in this situation, the quarterback wears a red shirt and is off-limits to tacklers. Not this time. The quarterbacks would get hit like everyone else . . . and Kemp was. The ligaments in his knee snapped and tore. He was finished for the season. Flores, as usual, also was hurt and so the quarterbacking job went by default to a rookie named Dan Darragh. Darragh, from William and Mary, was hardly a household word. He had been drafted in the 13th round. (Eventually, he, too, went down, and the Bills ended the season with running back Ed Rutkowski, who had not played the position since high school, at quarterback for the last three games.)

One more preseason game remained when Kemp was hurt. The Bills lost that one, then their opener to the Patriots, and next were embarrassed by Oakland (and Mr. Lamonica), 48–6. The next day Collier was fired as head coach. Harvey Johnson, the team's convivial head talent scout, was asked to take over. Johnson had no desire to coach, and, as he'd be the first to admit, he also had no real aptitude in that direction. But when the boss says, "Coach," you look for a blackboard and whistle. The season becomes a complete write-off with a 1–12–1 record—the worst in pro football. The team was a shambles, so was the organization. Morale was nonexistent, each player worried only about his own survival.

The only consolation was lead-off position in the draft. Many teams were willing to trade for this coveted spot, but Wilson spurned all offers. He wanted no more Daryle Lamonica embarrassments, and this year there was available a runing back from Southern Cal who figured to be an even bigger star. Ralph Wilson put his money on O.J. Simpson.

8

All the Wrong Numbers

Now that they had their No. 1 draft choice all signed and sealed, the Bills' front office began to worry as it became time for him to be delivered. How would Buffalo fans accept the man they felt had demeaned their city? According to the club, mail and phone calls generally had supported Wilson's stand in negotiations. The general tenor was, "Who the hell does he think he is?" In Buffalo much of the population carries a lunch bucket to work.

Simpson's flight from the West Coast was due to arrive about 9 P.M. The late Jack Horrigan, the Bills' vice-president in charge of public relations who would become one of O.J.'s closest friends and advisers, tried to keep the time secret, but news leaked out. As touchdown time neared, some 2,500 Buffalonians were on hand to greet the Juice. The mayor was among them. And a beauty queen to give him a kiss.

"I've been trying to get here for six months," Simpson began . . . and the crowd ate it up. Signing autographs, smiling, winking, making jokes, O.J. Simpson quickly folded Buffalo into the palm of his hand. Horrigan had a car and driver waiting for the 45-minute ride to training camp.

Buffalo fans weren't the only ones Simpson had to win over when he finally got to town. Even more important were his teammates, who could prove to be resentful not only of his high salary and attendant publicity but also of his late arrival. While Simpson had been negotiating and making lucrative personal appearances, they had been sweating out new coach John Rauch's tough two-a-days.

On his arrival Simpson had to take all the usual rookie hazing, including a rendition of his school fight song in the dining room. There was a little extra teasing about his fat contract, and the first few nights O.J. went out for beer with his new teammates they made sure he got the tab. This part he didn't mind a bit. O.J.'s entrée into pro football might have been a lot more difficult, except for the intervention of Tom Day, a veteran defensive end of boundless good humor. Day was the leader of the black players and a respected figure on the squad as a whole. He took O.J. under his wing early, and that saved Simpson a lot of possible misery. Veteran players exerted a lot of influence on the Bills.

There were problems getting Simpson suited up for his first workout.

In college he had worn No. 32—the same as Jim Brown—and a major star usually is allowed to keep his identifying number when he turns pro. But on the Bills a running back named Gary McDermott had been No. 32 the season before when he led the team in touchdowns as a rookie. McDermott wasn't about to surrender his jersey. "I think I earned it," he snapped when the question was raised, and for weeks the question was moot, because there was no Simpson on the grounds to dispute his claim.

The jersey issue could have created problems and resentment when Simpson did arrive, but he handled the matter diplomatically. "I'm here to play football not wear a jersey," he declared. "The whole thing is irrelevant."

When he made his pro debut that weekend he wore an unfamiliar No. 36, and this would be his designation through the rest of preseason until McDermott conveniently got himself cut the week before opening game.

More serious was the matter of a helmet. Simpson—remember his childhood nickname of "Headquarters"—could not comfortably or safely wear any of the helmets the Bills had in stock. It had something to do with the shape of his head, as well as the size. The standard suspension system in the Bills' style of helmets would have left him prey to concussions. For his first workouts Simpson practiced bareheaded until Southern Cal could air-freight one of his old hats to Niagara Falls (cost: $22) for temporary use. The Bills put in a rush order for a custom-made job, and general manager Bob Lustig shrugged off the difficulty. "We'll get him any kind of helmet he wants, just so he keeps it moving in the right direction."

During this awkward time Simpson made it a point to show some deference to another running back, Max Anderson. While McDermott figured to lose only a jersey, Anderson, who had led the team in rushing as a rookie the season before, figured to lose his job to the highly touted newcomer. Anderson stood only 5-8 and weighed 174 pounds. They called him Mini-Max, and he accepted Simpson's presence philosophically. "I can't hate him just because he's a great football player," Mini-Max declared.

As it turned out, Anderson, who had come to the Bills as a fifth-round draft choice out of Arizona State, carried the ball only 13 times in relief of Simpson in 1969. (He missed the whole next season with a knee injury, but then played two years in Canada after being cut by the Bills in 1971. In 1973, he failed to stick in tryouts with both the Chiefs and Patriots.)

Nobody was looking for omens at this point. Everyone was just glad to have O.J. Simpson aboard after his long holdout. But some of the opening statements from both Simpson and John Rauch were a bit disquieting as the rookie settled down to his new job.

On signing Simpson had said he thought he could be ready to play "in about three weeks." Rauch had other ideas. The Bills were booked for their third exhibition game of the season that Friday night in Detroit, and when O.J. reported for his first workout on Tuesday Rauch declared, "He will play in that game if we have to work with him 24 hours a day, which we'll probably have to."

Simpson had missed four important weeks of training camp, but Rauch was counting on O.J. to be in shape. Rauch felt the rookie's big problem would be mastering the complicated offensive system he had brought with him from Oakland.

The big adjustment, though, involved O.J.'s history of running the ball 30 to 40 times a game. At Southern Cal he had carried the Trojans' offense. As a highly paid No. 1 draft choice, he expected to be put to work the same way, or at least close to it. Why else were they paying him all that money?

Rauch was asked if this would be his plan, and he immediately bristled. "That's not my style," he snapped. "I couldn't build my offense around one back no matter how good he is. It's too easy for the pros to set up defensive keys."

He said Simpson also would be used as a pass receiver, and "we expect him to block, too."

The veteran quarterback, Jack Kemp, also expressed doubt that "you could run a back 30 times a game consistently in pro football." This feeling would prove to be significant, too, since Kemp liked to pass and had grown used to being allowed to call his own game on the field. (Kemp's philosophy and tendency to abandon a running game plan at the least excuse is what had led to the Cookie Gilchrist revolt some years earlier.)

However, there are few clairvoyants in football, or anywhere else, and so these omens generally were overlooked in the excitement of the moment as O.J. prepared for his professional debut. The crowd in Dertoit's Tiger Stadium numbered just over 34,000, and Lion officials estimated that perhaps 10,000 of these had decided to show up because of O.J. Simpson's advertised presence. Rauch didn't start him—he owed this much to Max Anderson and besides Simpson wasn't ready for that big a role. O.J. spent the first six minutes of his pro career on the bench before he finally entered the game, to bring in a play. Bills boosters thought it was highly significant that it produced a touchdown. The play was a 20-yard scoring pass from Tom

Flores to wide receiver Haven Moses. Simpson was open for a touchdown, too, but Flores didn't see him.

O.J., who hadn't really expected to play at all, didn't get back in the game (except to carry in another play) until the final period, when he saw some extended action. He had a 14-yard run, caught a 38-yard pass, failed to pick up one blitzing linebacker (groan), but did block another (cheers) to allow rookie quarterback Jim Harris to get off a TD pass. Detroit won, 24–12, but O.J., on the field for both Bills' touchdowns, was not displeased.

"I'm glad I've got that game behind me," he said, even though his body was bruised and sore, as Rauch had predicted it would be. O.J. hurt not so much from the game as from the cram course to get himself ready to play, and he had learned the hard way that running shape is not football shape. (It takes most running backs almost a week just to get their shoulders "set" before they can safely play.)

"I hadn't planned on using him as much as I did," Rauch admitted. "But he seemed to be enjoying it, and he gave me confidence that he knew his plays."

As the weeks went on, O.J. settled into the training routine, learning his plays, learning about his teammates. His roommate was Robert James, a free agent cornerback from Fisk University, so unsung that the Bills hadn't even bothered to include his name in their preseason press guide. No player from Fisk had ever made it in the pros.

The contrast between the two involved more than fame and finances. James came from Murfreesboro, Tennessee, and had attended a predominantly black college. This was his first real contact with the white world. On top of this he was fighting for his pro life every minute of the day, and for a Robert James this means more than just a chance to play football. His shot with the Bills was an opportunity to find a new world. Defensive and introverted, a small-town boy, he was hardly a match for the gregarious, big-city sophisticate who had just blown into town. It took many weeks and some sticky moments before the two finally drew close, personally and in a football sense. While James was getting to the point where he could savor the luxury and security of survival, Simpson was coming down to earth during a disappointing season. They met, from their two initial extremes, at what could be called the 50-yard line of life. Years later, as the only survivors of that rookie camp and the oldest Bills in point of service, they took special satisfaction in each other's success. Because Robert James became an all-pro, too.

After two more losses the Bills closed their exhibition schedule in Los Angeles before almost 70,000 fans, and the result was utter humiliation by a 50–20 score. More seeds of discontent were planted. O.J. carried only four times for 19 yards and caught three passes. Veteran players were miffed because, after the Bills' defensive unit had been introduced before the game, there was special recognition for Simpson on his old home field. "Where we come from, you introduce your offense or your defense. We got no room for superstars," snarled Deacon Jones of the Rams.

Pro football protocol may have been ignored in this case, but otherwise Simpson followed all the traditions. The night before the first regular-season game, Bills veterans would shave the heads of all the rookies who had survived the final squad cuts. It was a barber-ous way of acknowledging that the rookies had made it.

Simpson still was darting around the country on his time off for personal appearances, and he was in constant demand for television interviews. His appearance was important to him, but he had to undergo the ritual haircut along with the rest. O.J. took it more or less with a smile, but once he assumed a position of leadership he helped lead the fight to abolish this ritual that was unique to the Bills.

O.J.'s official pro debut as the most publicized college player in years was scheduled at home against the New York Jets, who had just shocked the world by upsetting Baltimore in the last Super Bowl. The Jets, of course, had their own superstar, Joe Namath.

Simpson's first pro game had to be rated as less than ordinary. By now he was the No. 1 halfback ahead of Mini-Max Anderson, but he carried the ball only 10 times for 35 yards, hauled a screen pass 55 yards for his biggest gain, and ran back kickoffs. One of his runs was eight yards for a touchdown and his teammates climbed all over him to offer congratulations when he scored. It was a typical O.J. run. "He gave me two inside fakes, then I thought he was going outside, but he came inside again," muttered Jet safety Jim Hudson, shaking his head.

The Bills lost the game, 33–19, but O.J. was able to chuckle quietly when they brought him his first real game check in the locker room, and he peered inside the envelope at all those zeroes. Potrero Hill never seemed farther away.

Simpson finally exploded in his third game. Against the

hapless Denver Broncos, coached by, yes, Lou Saban, he carried 24 times for 100 yards in a 41–28 victory, the Bills' first of the season. To O.J., sorely in need of a lift, it was a personal vindication. "I had been hearing so much about rookies can't do this and can't do that, I was beginning to believe it," he told Larry Felser of the Buffalo *Evening News*.

But if O.J. thought he was on the way, he would be bitterly disappointed. The 24 carries and 110 yards would be his highs for the season.

The next week he suffered a concussion in Houston despite his customized helmet and had to retire early, and he also was held out of the following Sunday's victory over Boston. He was back in the lineup, however, when the Bills returned to his hometown Bay Area to meet the Oakland Raiders.

This was an emotional return for Rausch as well as O.J., who admittely put extra effort into his game preparations. But the result was a second straight West Coast humiliation for both men. The Bills were crushed, 50–21, and O.J. carried the ball only six times. His single pass reception for the day came on a broken play. Most of the game he was used as a decoy.

Afterward, Simpson for the first time showed public anger and frustration.

"I was used less against Oakland than at any time in my career . . . high school, college or pro. I never got a chance to do much, and it's been that way all year. I'm not happy with my progress as a pro," he complained.

The defeat was Buffalo's fourth of the season, matching

the total number of times O.J. had been on the losing side since he left high school.

Simpson, of course, was aware that the Bills had fallen quickly behind by three touchdowns against the Raiders and thus were never in position to run the ball much. But he, and other pro football observers were beginning to wonder why Rauch seldom used him as a receiver. He'd been a good one in college, and although he admittedly was having trouble learning all his routes in the complicated Bills system, how smart did he have to be to catch a little swing pass that at least would get him out in the open field?

O.J.'s public blast helped bring to the surface a festering situation on the Bills. He and Rauch were the men in the middle because they were the new guys on the block.

Rauch, from Philadelphia, had been an all-America quarterback at the University of Georgia and later played pro ball with the Eagles. He got his first head coaching assignment when he moved up from an assistant's role at Oakland after Al Davis left for his brief stint as commissioner of the old American Football League. This was in 1966. Within months, Davis's aggressive moves had forced a merger with the NFL (with that league's Pete Rozelle remaining as overall commissioner). Davis resigned his post and returned to Oakland as "managing general partner." He would be a part-owner and operating head of the franchise while Rauch remained as head coach. However, with his own coaching background, Davis maintained an active interest in and control over the day-to-day operation of the Raiders. Rauch, a proud man, chafed under the constant supervision and resented comments that he was merely an Al Davis puppet.

Although he compiled a 33–8–1 record in three years as head coach and had taken the Raiders to the second Super Bowl, Rauch abruptly resigned after the 1968 season. Ralph Wilson, meanwhile, had been seeking for some weeks a full-time coach to succeed the interim Harvey Johnson. Even before Rauch quit at Oakland there were rumors he might be heading East, and as soon as his resignation became official, Wilson quickly hired him to bring order out of what had disintegrated in two short years into chaos.

When he got to Buffalo Rauch realized that the team he had inherited was a hollow shell. He knew a complete rebuilding was required, but he hesitated to act too quickly.

The veterans recalled the glory days of their recent championships, and they resented Rauch's efforts to sweep out their contemporaries. Lou Saban had hired all these guys and won with them. Joe Collier had gone to the wars with them, too, en route to championships, and the veterans actually had petitioned to get him the job when Saban left. Johnson was a happy spirit who had scouted and signed most of them and seldom worked them hard as coach. Now along came John Rauch who believed in a cold and distant approach to his players. The former quarterback was a technician, who carried with him also the alien Oakland philosophy that the quickest way to victory was not the run but the long pass. When he went surgically to work trimming away on the rotting football team he had been handed, there was open resentment.

Behind his back and as they sullenly sipped their beer after practice in a bar owned by Tom Sestak, a tackle who had just retired under pressure, and punter Paul Maguire, the players referred to Rauch as "Satan."

Simpson was shocked one night during his first training camp when drunken veterans went on a rampage and tore up the dormitory because a popular long-time substitute guard had just been cut. He would look on in dismay as the team continued to split during the season, the old guard against the new, defense against offense.

Soon after the Oakland debacle some of the veterans decided to hold a Hallowe'en costume party for the entire squad in an attempt to produce instant togetherness. It was a great party, but among the no-shows were the team's two captains, Harry Jacobs, a linebacker given to long-winded clubhouse speeches that turned O.J. and the other young players off, and Jack Kemp, the aging quarterback with a somewhat split personality. Part of him lived in the past when he could still whip the ball with authority, the rest already was living in the future and a career in politics. His conservative views in this area did little to endear him to young players just out of college.

The "old" Bills were a swashbuckling crew, the "new" were an intense generation reared on campus unrest. There was no middle ground. O.J. even noted that the hair styles were different and his wife Marguerite could feel the generation gap extending off the field as well. The families had little in common except their husbands' jobs.

There were many who thought O.J. might have provided some leadership, but he was in an ambiguous situation, too. Rookies are seen and not heard on a pro team, and he happened to be a rookie with a thick wallet and thin stats. Sure he was leading the Bills in rushing, but his 697 total yards would place him only sixth in the AFL, and his longest run would be a modest 32 yards. These were hardly the achievements of a No. 1 draft choice, and they did not entitle him to speak up in player councils.

Once, late in the season, O.J. did try to make some informal suggestions at the pregame meal as the Bills' offense went over its game plan. Finally, Butch Byrd, a cornerback who had been eavesdropping, blurted out, "Why don't you concentrate on your own job?" Simpson tried to think of an appropriate answer. "I still get my money," he said with a lame smile, but his teammates were not amused. By this time he also had alienated a lot of them with his constant references to Southern Cal and how his old teammates were doing en route to another big season.

Simpson's relationship with Rauch his rookie season was even worse. Rauch had played college ball under the late Wally Butts, an imaginative innovator in the passing game but also a hard-nosed disciplinarian who interspersed his tough workouts with a stream of profane abuse at his players. Rauch also was a screamer, albeit a lot more urbane, but his yelling irked Simpson, accustomed to the modish, wisecracking John McKay, who ran a generally loose ship.

"I just don't like to be yelled at," Simpson confessed one day.

"I don't think yelling is going to help much," he added. "But then I don't listen to it too much, anyway."

Tuning Rauch out was one thing, but turning his back on the coach while being lectured on pass routes, as he did one day in a fit of pique, was something else. O.J. skirted the boundary of insubordination as if he was dancing down the sidelines on one of his long college runs.

Simpson later admitted the back-turning incident was childish on his part and that he, too, was responsible for much of his rookie difficulty.

The first mistake was his long holdout. Whether it had been forced on him or not by Wilson's alleged stubbornness, it cost O.J. valuable time working with the team. The real heavy work in a pro camp is done in the first few weeks. Rauch was right in predicting it would take Simpson much longer to overcome the late start.

Barnes' eagerness to begin cashing in on Simpson's fame also hurt. There were the scores of deals to be considered and discarded, the few big ones to be signed, the dozens of appearances to be made for his various clients. They were lucrative, they were important for his future, but they kept O.J.'s mind off football. One major sports lawyer, Bob Woolf of Boston, says he seldom will sign business contracts for players (except those with short-term futures) right out of college. He reasons that it takes them a full year, often longer, to adjust to the new world and attitudes of pro sports. (Just hearing boos and reading a negative press for the first time proved upsetting to O.J., and he was not unique.)

Barnes, however, did not wait. He threw the ghetto kid immediately into the world of high finance. Later Simpson would admit: "My mind was not on football when I finally reported to camp. I just wasn't attuned to playing ball."

Too, when he did report, Simpson did not chuck his

outside interests. As soon as possible after a game, he'd be on a plane out of town to fulfill his various obligations, returning just in time to make Tuesday's practice. His teammates resented not so much his affluence from these appearances as the toll they knew it was taking on his concentration and his body. Instead of being cramped on airliners or on his feet signing autographs for salesmen's sons on Monday, he should have been stretched out in bed or in the whirlpool.

"He's a great runner," Butch Byrd said one day. "But he's going to have to decide whether he wants to be flying to Chicago or Detroit all the time to be on television, or play football. You have to dedicate yourself to this game."

O.J.'s presence and Rauch's organization (at least he was a professional coach in comparison to Johnson) did improve the Bills. They went from 1–12–1 to 4–10, but lost seven of their last nine games. In his final game of the season, O.J. carried only seven times in a 45–6 defeat in San Diego.

Carl Garrett of the Boston Patriots, a generally unheralded running back from New Mexico Highlands, had been picked on the third round of the pro draft, 57 players behind Simpson. When he signed he bragged publicly that he would beat out O.J. in voting for AFL Rookie of the Year. Everybody laughed at his bravado, but at season's end it was his turn to snicker. He was the AFL Rookie of the Year.

After the season Simpson made no secret of his frustration.

"I don't think I was a flop, I think the team was a flop," he told John Devaney. "At USC I was used to being beat up after a game. With Buffalo, I'd finish as fresh as when I started. When you feel that fresh, you don't feel you've played a game of football or done anything for your team."

Simpson was critical of Rauch's strategy and play-calling. "Let me run and Buffalo can be a winner," he proclaimed.

Simpson said he planned to report to training camp early the next summer with the rookies.

And he wrote his own definitive analysis of his first professional season. When Jack Horrigan asked him to list his accomplishments for the 1969 campaign on a postseason questionnaire given all players, Simpson was not being overly modest when he filled the space with one word in large print: "NONE."

9

"Years of Nothin'"

Everyone in the Bills' organization, including Simpson himself, spent the off-season analyzing O.J.'s rookie performance. With the merger completed, there was talk that the Juice might be traded to a West Coast team, like Los Angeles. Ralph Wilson even went so far as to suggest an even-up swap: O.J. to the Rams for quarterback Roman Gabriel.

L.A. Coach George Allen ignored him, but Gabriel was insulted. "The Rams should get more than just O.J. for me," he huffed.

Simpson went on tour for ABC Sports during the off-season telling all who asked, and possibly some who couldn't have cared less, that the Bills should use him more in 1970. He said that as a now-established second-year pro he felt more free to approach Rauch directly on this subject. He also would request that no more changes be suggested in his running style. He was tired of being criticized for the way he ran his sweeps. (The coaches claimed he turned upfield too quickly.)

O.J. also said he planned to report about 10 pounds heavier than the 207 at which he played the year before. Maybe he figured if Rauch turned down his bid to run the ball more he would need the weight for pass-blocking.

Confessing that he had waited a year too long, Rauch moved ruthlessly to clean house. Billy Shaw, Stew Barber, and Jack Kemp retired before training camp. Kemp that fall ran successfully as a Republican candidate for Congress. While campaigning he threatened his Buffalo constitutents that if he lost the election he would come back to play quarterback for the Bills. Tom Day, George Saimes, and Harry Jacobs, once defensive stalwarts, were released early. Al Bemiller got the message and retired. Booker Edgerson, another defensive fixture, was traded.

Rauch felt that all these old Bills had been playing on past reputation. "I went one year too long," the coach declared.

Some dissidents remained, however. Most notably these were punter Paul Maguire and defensive end Ron McDole, who represented the old guard, and the still-unhappy O.J. Simpson. Simpson and Rauch were just unable to establish any rapport.

Rauch is a decent, shy man, well liked by those who know him well, including this author. Too few of his players ever got the chance to know him well, though. They really didn't want to . . . and he in turn didn't make it easy for them. The most unfair accusation was that Rauch hobbled Simpson because of jealousy, that he didn't want his coaching overshadowed by Simpson's heroics. Anyone who knew Rauch realized this charge was ludicrous.

There's no question Rauch failed to exploit Simpson's talents. What he was trying to do was build a balanced football team in a classic sense. He was unwilling to use O.J. to buy him the time until this was accomplished, as Lou Saban would do when he took over.

Maybe he was wrong, but Rauch had his reasons.

"Remember, O.J. was averaging 30-some carries a game for Southern Cal," Rauch would point out later. "With that fine defense of theirs, they could afford to wait for O.J. to break the game open for them. But with Buffalo we'd get down by 14 points early, and we'd have to start playing catch-up. You can't play catch-up by giving the same guy the ball on every play and waiting for him to break one."

After O.J. broke all the records in 1973, the author wrote Rauch in Toronto where he was head coach of the Canadian League Argonauts. Rauch was asked to give his side of the O.J. controversy, and this is part of his reply:

"Some facts other than my coaching that held him back are:

"(1) O.J. was a great college player (Heisman Trophy), but like most college players entering the pro ranks, had a lot to learn about the pro game.

"(2) The publicity surorunding O.J.'s entry into pro ball put tremendous pressure on him to excel in his first year. This was made more difficult since the Bills were rebuilding from poor organization, bad facilities, and a losing atmosphere. . . .

"(3) O.J. and his agent were openly bitter to everything about Buffalo because they preferred the West Coast where his publicity could be marketed better. . . . It didn't help their feelings when Dennis Shaw was named Rookie of the Year in 1970, and this evidently led to a split on the team between Shaw fans and O.J. fans."

Dennis Shaw was a quarterback from San Diego State whom the Bills drafted on the second round, and by the third game of the regular season he had won the job. Shaw was blessed with a powerful arm and an eagerness to use it. In style he probably most resembled Daryle Lamonica, the former Buffalo quarterback, who had been so successful for Rauch in Oakland. Lamonica was known as the Mad Bomber. Shaw soon could be referred to as Son of Mad Bomber. After a holdout that lasted almost as long as O.J.'s the year before, he quickly established himself as one of the brightest quarterback prospects in football.

Rauch thus finally had his strong-armed quarterback to implement the passing game he loved so well. O.J. and the rushing offense again became secondary. (There is no hard evidence that any Shaw-Simpson rivalry existed or that it split the team. Most of the players were too busy hating Rauch. The division could have been in the coach's own mind as he himself pondered the contrasting styles each represented.)

The new rookie crop did, however, provide one solace for Simpson. Al Cowlings, his boyhood friend, had developed into an outstanding defensive lineman for Southern Cal. The Bills picked him on the first round.

For all of O.J.'s off-season enthusiasm, the Bills started the new year more dismally than they had ended the previous campaign. They dropped five of six exhibition games and their first two in regular season. O.J. looked so frustrated in the opener against Denver that Bronco running back Floyd Little was moved to call him aside after the game. "Don't worry, my first two years at Denver were terrible," Little said. "It takes time to build a line. Hang in there, your time will come."

In a wide-open game the Bills beat the Jets, 33–31, as O.J. gained 99 yards. Two more losses followed, but then the Bills rebounded with consecutive victories over the Jets and Patriots. Against the Pats, Simpson ran for a career high of 123 yards and a 7.2 average. Maybe at last he and the Bills with a first-half 3–4 record were on their way.

Going into the eighth game of the season, O.J. had gained 448 yards, which projected to just short of 1,000 for the year. With a little luck, he might make it.

Game 8 was at home against the Cincinnati Bengals, who had lost six in a row. The favored Bills led 7–3 and again at 14–13 on Simpson's one-yard touchdown run. But then Lemar Parrish scored on a 95-yard kickoff return, and Horst Muhlmann kicked a field goal for a 23–14 Bengal lead just before the half.

Now it was up to Muhlmann to kick off again with only seconds remaining before the intermission. All Simpson could think of was breaking a long return so the Bills would carry some momentum into the dressing room. O.J. was leading the league in kickoff returns, so Muhlmann tried to aim the ball away from him, but Simpson caught up with it after a long run and headed upfield. Muhlmann, a German-born soccer kicker, was the first man to grab the Juice, but as O.J. tried to break away, more Bengal tacklers came slamming into him.

O.J.'s left leg was planted in the turf, and his knee

twisted as he went down. Two teammates, one Al Cowlings, had to carry him off the field.

The Bills were dead for the rest of the game, and, as it proved, for the season.

For some reason it took several weeks before Simpson's injury was finally diagnosed. Almost a month after he was hurt, the team doctor declared him done for the season. The injury was described as a slight tear in the tissue behind the left knee. No operation would be necessary, the wound would heal itself. But by the time it did, the season would be over. O.J., who had not played since he was hurt, might as well go home.

The Juice had never made any secret of his eagerness to return to California after the season. Buffalo still was not home to him, nor to his wife. Marguerite and their two small children, Arnella and Jason, usually would head home to set up housekeeping in Bel Air a week or two before the season ended. Asked about this once, O.J. explained, "I guess she got tired of Niagara Falls. You see one waterfall, you've seen 'em all."

But Simpson never anticipated having to go home this early or under these conditions. He was weary and in pain and depressed. And obviously fearful as well. Who knows if he wouldn't need an operation later on before he could play? Knee injuries had ended more than one football career. He would not know for sure for more than six months, when he took some knocks in training camp.

With Simpson gone, the Bills disintegrated. From the moment he was helped off the field they lost every game, seven in a row. Their 3–10–1 record marked absolutely no progress. Even though he had missed almost half the season, Simpson still ended up as the Bills' leading ground gainer.

Rauch, through this stretch, lost almost complete touch with the team. The Bills were in virtualy open revolt, and for this the coach could not blame Simpson's poor attitude. Rauch had just completed the first half of a four-year contrast. If he was to survive, he would need the complete backing of management. There were indications from those close to the team that he did not have this critical support from the front office and from Wilson. They were losing confidence in him, too.

Wilson, however, had other things on his mind. For years he had been trying to get Buffalo-Erie County to agree on building a new stadium to replace antiquated War Memorial. The old facility was a decrepit pile of stone situated in one of Buffalo's most decayed areas. Parking facilities were nil, and the stadium, despite an earlier expansion, did not reach NFL requirements of 50,000 seats. The locker rooms, especially those for visiting teams, were a disgrace. Fans or workers stuck in the stadium after dark left in groups.

Whenever progress on a new stadium stalled, which was frequent, Wilson would threaten to move his team to Seattle. Simpson didn't exactly endear himself to Buffalo fans when he was quoted to the effect that this might not be a bad idea. He said a lot of other players wouldn't mind it, either. "If I was Ralph Wilson, I'd move," he declared.

Simpson later tried to explain that he was only trying to show that he and all the players were solidly behind Wilson's campaign to get a new stadium. He said he loved playing in Buffalo, but was not too convincing.

The stadium was taking all of Wilson's time. He couldn't worry about the coaching.

During the off-season, though, a strange change began to take place among the Bills. As they spent the lonely winter at home—losers aren't often invited out—they began to think, think seriously. Maybe Rauch wasn't the source of their problems. None of those supposedly great veterans he had cut had gone to other teams with any success. Rauch certainly had been a winner with Oakland. The players knew they had not been fair to him. Maybe he deserved a real chance.

As one anonymous veteran told sportswriter Jim Peters, "I spent the entire off-season thinking about our situation and finally realized that the trouble wasn't Rauch, nor his system, but our refusal to work with him."

There were further indications that this veteran was not alone in his thinking. The Bills were prepared to come to training camp for the first time in years as a team.

During that same off-season Rauch made two more moves to sever the past. Paul Maguire, the free spirit punter, was released, and Ron McDole, another old pro, was traded to Washington, where he found new life as a member of George Allen's Over the Hill Gang.

On a television interview as camp opened, Rauch was asked about the two departed veterans. He referred to Maguire as the "team clown," and he said that McDole hadn't "played what in my standards is winning football the last three years."

Wilson soon heard of Rauch's comments, and they seemed to unleash all the resentment that apparently had been festering within him the last two years. Wilson, too, personally identified with the glory years of the Bills, and he could not bear public disparagement of the men who had bled and won for him. He stormed into the Niagara Falls training base and informed Rauch that he planned a public "defense" of the two players.

Rauch had been unnecessarily tactless in his remarks, but this slip probably stemmed from his belief that Maguire and McDole had tried to undermine him. But Wilson's threat was indefensible. Rauch knew it . . . and maybe, just maybe, Wilson knew it, too.

"If you make that statement, I will resign," Rauch told his owner.

"I accept your resignation," Wilson replied.

And so, for the second time in four years, John Rauch walked out on a head coaching job in the NFL. He may not have been the world's greatest coach or its most charismatic personality, but none of the dissident Bills could deny his stubborn courage.

Later, referring obviously to this incident and the climate that produced it, Rauch would say of Lou Saban's take-over of the Bills: "I think he'll get the job done right because he'll be allowed to do it his own way. I didn't have that freedom, and that was my downfall." Of course, part of coaching is getting that authority, by force of personality even if it's not written into the contract. In his letter about O.J.'s early years, Rauch wrote: "I admit to some mistakes as coach of the Bills . . . [who] have improved their organization by giving Saban the control a coach needs."

What the Bills saw in the next five months persuaded them that if Rauch wasn't the best football coach in North America, he was far from the worst.

In any two-man race that honor would go to good ol' Harvey Johnson who, for the second time in four years would try to overlook what it did to his stomach and loyally heed Ralph Wilson's call to ride to the rescue. He ended up doing slightly worse than the first time around, dropping from 1–12–1 to 1–13. For the second time in four years, the Bills would be the worst team in football.

Bills' players probably realized before Wilson what a terrible mistake had been made. Johnson was a likable guy, a good talent scout, but his training camp was a joke. Two-a-day drills in blistering summer heat when players are just starting to get into shape can be a retching experience. When the Bills finished a Johnson two-a-day, they'd go out and play basketball to work off their excess energy.

One of Rauch's faults as a coach had been his attempt to exercise complete control over every phase of the operation. When he left none of his holdover assistants was equipped to help Johnson run things.

The Bills went out and lost their first 10 games before finally defeating a similarly disorganized New England Patriot team, 27–24. Although armed with one of pro football's best runners in Simpson, a strong-armed passer in Dennis Shaw, and great receivers in Haven Moses and Marlin Briscoe, the Bills were shut out four times, including twice by Baltimore. At one point they went 10 straight quarters without scoring. Their first shutout loss to the Colts was by a score of 43–0 and O.J. was held to *minus*-10 yards. He called it one of the most humiliating experiences of his life.

"We played the worst game since I've been with this team," he declared. "When I first came to Buffalo we didn't have half the talent we have now. . . . I can't understand how things could be so bad. We had receivers open all day, but how can the quarterback throw the ball when he's on his back? We started out with missed assignments on each of our first four plays, and things got worse from there."

Even Wilson had to admit his disillusionment. "We're just disorganized," he said. "We play like the College All-Stars against the professional champions."

Simpson once again led the Bills in rushing with 742 yards on a game high of 106 against San Diego. That game, of course, had been played out on the Coast. He summed up the season in one word: "Terrible."

Looking back on his brief career, Simpson could see that the Bills had gone from four victories to three to one. This was not exactly progress. The past season had been a complete write-off and apparently one accepted by management, when it forced the Rauch confrontation at the time it did. If the Bills had been working on some plan, some pattern for building, Simpson would not have been so discouraged by all the losses.

He made his decision as Buffalo struggled through its lost season. He would not return to the Bills unless the team made some commitment to winning.

Three years gone from those glory days at Southern Cal, O.J. was facing the fourth and final season of his contract, although he still would be obligated for a fifth "option" campaign. As the 1971 season wound down, Simpson speculated openly that he would play the five years and quit pro football. He would take up the TV and movie career for which ABC had been grooming him, he hinted.

The strategy was obvious. He would force Ralph Wilson to trade him, preferably westward, before his final contract season. Wilson was astute enough to know that if he waited until O.J.'s contract was about to expire, he would be dealing from weakness. He would get more value if he traded a Simpson who still had two years to go on an operative contract. The ultimate threat, of course, was that O.J. would outright quit. Then Wilson would end up with nothing but an empty locker and an outsized helmet that wouldn't fit anyone else.

"I'd just had three years of nothin'," O.J. related some time later, "and I knew that while they might have some trouble trading me, there were teams that were interested. Heck, I had no big love for the city, and the city had no big love for me. I'd passed the point where I was a drawing card in Buffalo, or anyplace else for that matter, because of the three wasted years. I had no plans to play out my option, and if they didn't trade me I was going to resort to other tactics, which I don't want to mention. Fortunately, it never got that far. But when I left Buffalo after the 1971 season, I had no plans to play there the next year."

Simpson's feelings were well known within the Bills' family, but fortunately O.J. had Jack Horrigan as a friend. Horrigan was more than just a publicity man with the Bills, he was privy to executive decisions. His advice to O.J. over the years had been good, and the Juice was convinced that Horrigan had his interests at heart. They visited socially, and, as O.J. would get more and more worked up over his frustration in Buffalo, Horrigan counseled patience.

"Just wait, just wait," the former newspaperman would say soothingly to the distraught star.

Something was in the works, Horrigan hinted, something that would turn the Bills' program and O.J.'s career onto the right track.

"Horrigan was my man," O.J. explained later. "When he told me what was happening, I promised I'd give it another year."

10

"We're Going to Give You the Ball"

What Jack Horrigan knew was that delicate negotiations were under way to bring Lou Saban back to Buffalo. Neither Saban nor the Bills had been very happy or successful since the divorce.

Saban had gone to Maryland under a four-year contract calling for $25,000 annually and in his first season had produced a 4–6 record. However, he soon learned the college scene was not as idyllic as he had remembered it. The pressures of recruiting were even greater than they had been with the pros. On top of this, right after he left, the two professional leagues declared peace and instituted a common draft. No longer would coaches have to wine, dine, and hide out college seniors just for the chance to offer them outrageous sums of money.

Saban and his family were not unhappy in College Park, Maryland, but they still were receptive when Gerry Phipps, president of the Denver Broncos, came calling. Phipps' team had just wound up another dismal season under an interim coach, and he was prepared to offer Saban complete control if he would undertake to build it into a winner. Phipps said he was thinking in terms of a five-year contract.

"Too bad it's not 10," Saban said, half in jest.

"Fine," said Phipps, and Saban was hooked.

"The long-term proposition outweighed the pleasures of college life," Saban said as he announced his departure. Maryland officials would not hold him to the remaining three years of his contract. The Broncos would double his salary to $50,000 annually, and he would also be the general manager.

For all his previous success in Buffalo, Saban was doomed to failure in Denver, a charter member of the American Football League that had never enjoyed a single winning season. The Broncos had started out mismanaged and underfinanced. When the wealthy Phipps brothers took over the ownership, money was no problem, but Denver's isolated position was. Top college prospects preferred to play in the bigger cities, and during the war they had that alternative. When the merger was completed, the Broncos found themselves in what was then pro football's toughest division where they had to go home-and-home each season with Oakland, Kansas City, and San Diego. The only thing that ended Denver's lease on last place was the arrival of Cincinnati as an expansion team.

Thus, despite his feverish efforts to transform the Broncos, Saban found himself running on a treadmill. He was like the last runner on a relay team taking over the baton two laps in arrears. Under Saban the Broncos took two major strides forward. The stadium was enlarged, thus ending continuous speculation that the franchise would be moved. And he signed Floyd Little and then developed the Syracuse All-America into Denver's first 1,000-yard rusher. The latter development would end up helping him more in Buffalo than in Denver.

The Broncos' record during Saban's five years bore an embarrassing sameness: 3–11, 5–9, 5–8–1, 5–8–1, 4–9–1. Whatever progress the team may have been making was not visible . . . but Saban was. As in his previous stops, the strong-willed coach continued his philosophy of "do something, even if it's wrong." And so the focus of fan discontent centered on his broad shoulders. Saban found himself the target of unmatched personal vilification in Denver. The windows of his home were broken, garbage was dumped on his front lawn. His four children were abused in school. His own health began to suffer.

Saban, of course, still had his 10-year contract, but in the middle of his fifth season the Phipps brothers, too, appeared to be growing uncomfortable.

On November 17, 1971, with five gamess to go, Saban announced his resignation as head coach. Line coach Jerry Smith took over the team on an interim basis, and Saban remained as general manager. At the time he said his main job as GM the rest of the year would be to find a permanent successor to coach and run the team. During this period he and Ralph Wilson again made contact. The rumors of his return to Buffalo began then.

On December 19, Floyd Little gained 79 yards against Oakland to win the NFL rushing championship. On December 22, Saban's resignation as GM was announced with more speculation that he would be going back to Buffalo. The very next day he arrived on the shores of Lake Erie, and the second coming became official. He was given a 10-year contract to be vice president in charge of football and head coach. Bob Lustig continued as general manager, but with business responsibilities only. Buffalo fans were overjoyed.

Saban, of course, having been in the league, knew the Bills' shortcomings. He recognized that O.J. Simpson was the team's major, and perhaps only, asset. The champions Saban had left behind six years earlier were only a memory, best forgotten except on old-timer's day.

Although his coaching pride prevents him from admitting it outright, Saban had to be aware that his first task as coach was to get Simpson on his side. O.J. by now was the bellwether of the team, and his poor relationship with Rauch had helped make that man's position untenable. Saban would not bend for Simpson, but he had a feeling they were both on the same wavelength and his job was to communicate this to O.J.

"Offenses and defenses have to tie themselves around certain players," Saban would explain later. "They have to have a hub and then, one by one, the other players become the spokes."

O.J. would be the hub of his offense and, as he performed well, the others would develop pride and, hopefully, a winning attitude.

Both Saban and Simpson independently made plans to attend the Hula Bowl. Simpson was going to assist on ABC's telecast. Saban, accompanied by his wife, was on a half-vacation, half-scouting trip. They were booked out on separate flights, but just before takeoff O.J.'s plane developed a malfunction, and the airline changed its booking. He found himself virtually across the aisle from Lou Saban, another of those little coincidences that have marked his life.

As their flight headed across the Pacific, Simpson and his new coach got to know each other. They talked football. Saban expounded his philosophy and how it would apply to O.J. His basic message to O.J. was simple. "Report to camp in shape, because we're going to give you the football."

Saban emphasized that he believed in the running game. "It may take time," he promised. "But I'm going to get quality linemen to block for you."

Saban explained that even when Simpson was being called upon to block, catch passes, or act as a decoy, he would be setting up situations that might help him break a long run. "But we won't use you to block too much, because we'll want you running with the ball," the coach added with a wink.

Even Saban's plan to rebuild the Buffalo defense, his trademark with the winning Bills, was related to the run and O.J. "We need a defense that will get the ball back for you," he pointed out.

"We know you're a great running back, and we're going to give you the ball as often as we can," Saban repeated, but he also stressed that this would not be a one-way relationship. He expected a lot from Simpson in return.

"I expect you to produce," Saban said grimly, "and I expect you to become a team leader."

All through his career before he turned pro, Simpson

had been a team captain. He welcomed the responsibility again with the Bills, especially when he looked up late in training camp the next summer and realized that he was one of the most experienced players on the squad. Never a speechmaker, Simpson thought he could lead the team as a "doer," his word. When he did speak up, he knew the players would listen. And he knew he could relay their complaints to the front office without fear of being put on waivers the next day.

Even before their first meeting, Simpson was well aware of Saban's reputation. He had checked him out. He knew how Cookie Gilchrist had starred for Saban in Buffalo and how Floyd Little had become a star for him in Denver. The previous season Simpson had averaged 4.1 yards a carry to 3.0 for Little. But Little carried the ball 101 times more and so led the league with 1,133 yards. O.J.'s total was 742.

Simpson also knew that he and Saban shared a philosopsy that football is a physical game in which manhood is involved. To this kind of coach or player, there is beauty in the off-tackle plunge and something almost effete in the passing game that sees potbellied quarterbacks playing catch with ballet-dancer wide receivers. Don Shula of the Miami Dolphins spoke eloquently for this school when he noted, "Running puts the man in football." (Characteristically, coaches like Saban and Shula also stress rugged defense.) Even line blocking up front illustrates the Saban/Shula theory. Pass blockers must be passive types, conditioned to absorbing blows as they slowly give ground. Blocking for the run requires an aggressive charge, the dealing out of blows. Most linemen prefer to block for the run where they can finally dish it out.

Saban is a physical man and so his football philosophy was an extension of self. Simpson, who remembered when "the best athlete was the leader of the gang," could understand.

"A quarterback can do more for a team statistically, but mentally a running back can do more because the guys can better identify with a running back," Simpson explained one day. "At one time in their careers all football players ran with the ball, but not too many of them played quarterback."

"It's a manliness thing, too," O.J. continued, warming to his subject. "Many quarterbacks are not 'physical,' but most football players are, and so they further identify with running backs, who have to hit people, too. Look in the past at the names most football players respect—Bronco Nagurski, Red Grange. They're running backs. I think one reason players respect a quarterback like Joe Namath is that they can see that before he got his knees hurt, he was a runner and a good athlete who wasn't afraid of getting hit. Our Joe Ferguson will run with the ball and take his knocks, too, which is why the guys respect him."

Simpson was not afraid of dividing the team if Saban loaded the offense on his shoulders. He was confident he could carry it off.

"When a guy can be accepted as the best, like, boom, all the guys playing with him say, 'Hey, we got the best running back in the game on our side' and they feel better about themselves and what they're playing with. Look at what Joe Namath does for the Jets. Even the defense plays better when he's in there. It's an unbelievable thing, but because everybody knows Joe's the best and because Joe's on their side, they play better. It's like when you're growing up and playing in the park, the same guys always played better when they were on my side."

Simpson felt the Bills were just overdue in their decision to let him carry the offense. "Look, the Buffalo Bills had their choice of any football player in the country, and they drafted me No. 1 as a runner," he pointed out. "Then, when they got me, they acted like they wanted me to do everything except run, except what they drafted me for and what I wanted to be, a runner."

As their plane touched down in Hawaii, Simpson and his new coach made a date to meet for dinner a couple of nights later. Saban said he wanted to hear O.J.'s thoughts about what was wrong with the Bills and what suggestions he might have for improving the situation.

O.J. showed up at the restaurant at the appointed hour, but Saban did not appear. Simpson is a proud man, but his reaction when he next got to Buffalo showed that he already had accepted Saban as the boss. "Is the coach upset with me? Did I say something wrong on the plane?" O.J. asked Jack Horrigan. Only then did Simpson learn that Saban had been stricken with a serious gall bladder attack soon after they had arrived. The coach eventually underwent surgery, and his early staff meetings as he took over the Buffalo operation were held in Denver, where he was confined through his recovery.

Once again the Bills had first choice in the pro draft, and Saban opted for defense, choosing Notre Dame lineman Walt Patulski on the opening round. But leading off the second cycle, he made a nod in O.J.'s direction by choosing Reggie McKenzie, a huge all-America guard from Michigan. McKenzie, a magnificent physical specimen at 6-4, 240, would become Simpson's closest friend and eventual roommate. O.J. quickly recognized something special in the rookie because he took him under his wing—the way Tom Day had done for him—and he helped McKenzie blossom in the alien Buffalo atmosphere.

It is not strange that the two have become friends. They are a lot alike. McKenzie, almost as articulate, has great pride, too. He stresses that when he reported to his first training camp, "O.J. had to win my respect, too, as a running back and as a man." (He leaves no doubt that he passed this test in a hurry, and now his admiration for O.J. is total, as a running back and as a man, "a helluva man.") McKenzie, like Simpson, also has a great sense of team obligation. While in college, Reggie shared a house with six other football players. They called it "The Den of the Mellow Men." After he made All-America, McKenzie was honored by his home town of Highland Park, Michigan. He insisted that the other "Mellow Men" share the platform with him, and when he stood up to speak he first introduced his closest college chums to the crowd, adding a little personal note about each. Bob Lustig, GM of the Bills, was present and recalls how impressed he was with McKenzie's gesture.

The drafting of McKenzie wasn't Saban's only signal to Simpson that he planned to shore up the running game. When the Bills reported to camp, the wide receivers discovered that full linemen's "cages" had replaced the two protective face-bars on their helmets. They would be required to block like everyone else, and Saban pointed out that if they could master the devastating crackback block and free Simpson on some end sweeps they would be putting money in their own pockets.

Marlin Briscoe, who had taxied under Saban as a quarterback in Denver, played out his option, and the new coach let him depart to Miami. Haven Moses was a gifted receiver, but he showed little inclination to block and he soon departed. The Bills ended Saban's first year with two new wide receivers who had won their jobs by knocking people down, J.D. Hill, who also could fly and catch the ball, and Bob Chandler, who had played with O.J. at Southern Cal.

By the time he reported to camp, Simpson was wildly enthusiastic about his prospects and those of the team under Saban. The men had talked often during the off-season, and always Saban's message was the same: "Be ready, we're going to give you the football."

There remained, however, one potential problem. The last year of Simpson's original contract was coming up, and O.J. knew that wherever he went during the season he would be asked if he planned to play out his option the following year and jump to another team. Although he insisted later he had never publicly "asked to be traded," he was dealing with semantics. He had never masked his feeling that Buffalo was not his favorite city.

O.J. also had never completely hidden his opinion of Rauch, and he knew writers all year would be asking pointed questions about his relationship with Saban.

He and Jack Horrigan talked about these potential trouble spots many times. It was Horrigan who suggested that the solution might be a new contract. Simpson said that he felt he deserved a raise anyway, and so the low-key Horrigan suggested innocently, "Well, why don't you talk to Lou about it?"

(Later Simpson would chuckle, "Yeah, and I bet Jack was talking to Lou then, too, and telling him 'Hey, why don't you talk to O.J. about a new contract?' ")

Soon after he reported to camp Simpson requested an audience with his new coach.

As they sat down—Simpson significantly unaccompanied by agent or lawyer—O.J. came right to the point.

"You know," he said, "I'm sure every place I go this year people will ask me 'Are you going to play out your option?' Well, I don't want to play out my option, and I don't want all this distraction. I want to concentrate on just what we have to do here, and I'd like to discuss an extension of my contract now and have it over with."

Within 15 minutes after O.J.'s little speech, terms of a new four-year contract, starting immediately and superseding the old agreement, had been hammered out. Wilson was informed, and a public announcement made. All hands, including Buffalo fans, were jubilant. After all the smart remarks, here was a man voluntarily sentencing himself to four more years in their town. It was a great boost to civic pride.

Here's how Simpson explains his decision to seek the extension:

"For one thing, I wanted more money. And, let's face it, Lou Saban, as a new coach, and I were on shaky ground. The new team couldn't have worked if I wasn't happy. Everybody in Buffalo was talking to me about playing out my option, and here he was a new coach trying to set a new tone, a new mood with a new organization. Obviously I was going to be a main cog in this new mood, and it would be tough playing a season trying to get in a new spirit with every day people asking me if I was going to play out my option and then what?

"To kind of kill a lot of that and to let everyone know I was dedicated to the program and had belief in Lou Saban, this is what we decided to do. Although the next year would have been my option year, that season (1972) would have been the big year. If I hadn't signed, I would have sat out because I can make money doing other things. It wouldn't have come to that, but it [the new contract] was just something that had to be done."

Understanding this emotional and dramatic background, it is easy to see why Ralph Wilson at season's end would credit Saban's quick establishment of rapport with O.J. for keeping the running back in a Buffalo uniform. And why Simpson would say of Saban with deep feeling, "He saved my career."

There were other factors involved in O.J.'s decision to link his future with the Bills. Over the years he had developed some strong friendships on the team and a feeling of identity when he ran out on the field in his blue jersey and white helmet adorned on each side with a red buffalo.

As he put it at the press conference announcing his contract extension: "I cried with these guys who are my teammates. Someday I want to drink champagne with them."

Also, almost imperceptibly, Simpson had found himself developing a feeling of community with the city of Buffalo.

He'd never spend his winters there, but he just seemed to have awakened one autumn morning feeling at home. With a new maturity he became aware that his constant discontent with the environment had contributed to his poor play. "I realized it was time to stop thinking about playing out my option, getting traded, running away. Whatever I might have thought earlier, I had to accept the Bills as my team."

McKenzie, as he talked with O.J. about the past and saw his friend's new acceptance of the present, could see how this change in attitude was helping Simpson's performance. "He finally accepted that Buffalo was where his job was," McKenzie noted.

For the first time in his pro career, Simpson would be playing real home games. Buffalo fans, who had been waiting with growing impatience and skepticism for O.J. to deliver on his Heisman Trophy promise, quickly noticed the change and took him to their hearts.

As the new season began, however, it seemed as if the fates had conspired to play a cruel joke on O.J. Simpson. One after another his offensive linemen went down with injury. Second-, third- and fourth-string guards and centers were rushed into service and just as quickly assisted limping off the field. The Bills felt their team doctor should have given them a flate rate on knee operations. Linemen would be culled off the waiver wire one week, start the next, and spend the third in the hospital recuperating from surgery. At one point in the huddle to start a game, O.J. suggested to the linemen, "Take off your helmets and introduce yourselves to each other."

At various times he played behind four different centers,

five different tackles, and ten different guards. When the season ended, four offensive linemen who had been starters briefly during the season were released on waivers. One game the Bills used an unbalanced line with three tackles and one guard.

It may have seemed like the discouraging old times as the Bills opened at home with a 41–24 loss to the Jets. The Bills fell three touchdowns behind in the first half, and O.J. carried only 14 times all day for a net of 41 yards.

A week later the San Francisco 49ers came to town. This was the team O.J. and his friends had sneaked into Kezar Stadium to watch and, at the beginning, Simpson and Al Cowlings were properly awed.

"It was unreal," O.J. said afterward. "I'm out there with guys Al and I used to jump the fence to watch. We were real 49er fans, believe me. We never missed a game. Sometimes we'd get in on a pass, but we'd always find a way."

On this afternoon in Buffalo O.J. did find a way, and for the first time in his pro career he saw what the future could be. Twenty-nine times he carried the ball, his professional high, and when they toted up his production it came to 138 yards. Not since he wore the Cardinal and Gold of Southern Cal had he gained so many yards. He didn't score any touchdowns, but that was all right. Jim Braxton, the 243-pound fullback, tallied a pair on short plunges in the final period as Buffalo rallied for a 27–20 victory over one of the NFL's quality elevens.

As the hometown crowd of more than 45,000 roared its approval, O.J. had to agree that the future looked very pleasant indeed, despite the disastrous run of injuries.

Five weeks later the Bills came up against the rock-hard

Pittsburgh Steelers. Saban, improvising frantically, devised his unbalanced line in an attempt to nullify the Steelers' great tackle, Mean Joe Greene. The Steelers won the game, 38–21, but they never stopped the Juice, who gained a new career high of 189 yards. He averaged 8.6 a carry.

It was now halfway through the season, and O.J. had gained 678 yards. Before the first game Simpson had said that he hoped to make 1,500. That figure now seemed out of reach, thanks to all the injuries, but O.J. still had his shot at 1,000. Onward he drove, with Reggie McKenzie, the rookie who played like a man, and Dave Foley just about the only constants in his offensive line. No wonder O.J. kept Reggie around all the time. He wanted to make sure he stayed healthy.

By game 10, in which he gained 103 yards against the Patriots, Simpson had 915 yards.

The next week the Bills went to Cleveland to play the Browns. Simpson was singularly thrilled when he saw that many Buffalo fans who had driven over for the game had decorated the stadium with banners exhorting him to make his 1,000. It was quite a change in one year.

Simpson scored early on a six-yard run as the Bills took a 10–0 first-quarter lead. But then the Browns, in the midst of a late-season hot streak that would carry them to the playoffs, tied in the second period. They went ahead in the third quarter on a touchdown set up by O.J.'s fumble.

Cleveland scored 10 more points in the final period to lead by 17, and with the game out of reach O.J.'s teammates decided to let Juice go for his 1,000. Again and again they gave him the ball, and on his last carry he went over 1,000 by eight yards.

Larry Brown of the Redskins had made his 1,000 the week before, but Simpson was the first player in the AFC to reach that plateau.

Baltimore held O.J. to only 26 yards the following week, but the next Sunday he exploded for 116 in a 21–21 tie with Detroit to break Cookie Gilchrist's 1962 club record of 1,096.

At this point, with a game to go, Simpson had 1,150 yards, best in the American Conference. Larry Brown led the National Conference and the NFL overall with 1,216. In the final game of the season, the two would meet head-to-head in Washington's Robert F. Kennedy Stadium.

But the confrontation was not to be. Brown had missed the previous game with a leg injury. He still was hurting and, because the Redskins already were assured of their spot in the playoffs, Washington coach George Allen elected to hold out his star halfback for another week.

As the Bills closed their season with a 24–17 upset victory, O.J. carried the ball 26 times for 101 yards. His final season total was 1,251, the best in pro football.

But, to O.J. Simpson, the victory was hollow. Something was missing. Whenever he refers to the 1972 season, it is as "the year I led the NFL in rushing when Larry Brown missed the last two games."

11

Going for Two Grand

Although his 1,000-yard season and NFL rushing title were not as satisfying as they might have been, O.J. Simpson's fourth pro campaign was not without its rewards.

He was chosen almost unanimously as the AFC's Player of the Year, and for the second time in his career he got to play in the All-Star game.

The first occasion had been after his rookie year, the last time the AFL and NFL held separate games. O.J.'s college reputation was still fresh, and there is evidence he was named to the East squad mainly to help the gate in Houston. The next two years O.J. would go out to the Pro Bowl camps in Los Angeles and wistfully watch the workouts like a kid with his nose pressed to the window of a neighborhood bakery.

The Pro Bowl following the 1972 season was held in Dallas, and unlike his previous post-season appearance in Texas, this time O.J. was present on his merits. Veteran pros generally are less than enthusiastic about the Pro

Bowl. Those that don't find an excuse to drop out use the occasion for a week-long party. (One player has called the game "twenty-two guys with a hangover leaning against each other.") However, to first-time selectees, it's quite a thrill, and O.J. had been out in the cold too long.

Approaching the game with enthusiasm, he scored a touchdown by breaking five tackles on a six-yard run, caught three passes, and gained 112 yards on only 16 carries. The AFC won, 33–28, and Simpson was named the game's most valuable player. All-star teammate Mean Joe Greene was moved to comment, "Man, if that guy had some blocking in Buffalo they'd have to ban him from the league."

Within a week the Bills moved to get him that blocking in the annual college draft. Although the Bills' 1972 record was only 4–9–1, it was their best finish since 1966 and, most encouraging, Simpson at last could see signs of an organization and a plan for improvement. Still, the record was poor enough to provide Buffalo with a favorable position in the draft.

Picking seventh among 26 teams, the Bills for their first choice selected Paul Seymour, a 6-5, 255-pound tackle from the University of Michigan. Then, with another first-round choice obtained from Miami in payment for Marlin Briscoe, the Bills tabbed a second offensive lineman, 254-pound Michigan State guard Joe DeLamielleure.

Lou Saban was making good on his promise to put together that quality line.

(In the third round as the 57th player in the nation, the Bills went for quarterback Joe Ferguson, but at this point few paid much attention because the once-promising

Arkansas prospect had not enjoyed a very good senior year.)

As training camp neared the Bills received a major scare: DeLameilleure flunked his physical because of a suspected heart condition. It looked as if he would never be able to play football again, and he was resigned to the fact. But additional tests cleared him to play. Another apparent setback was turned into a plus. Jan White, the regular tight end, abruptly quit football so the rookie Seymour was moved out to fill his position. This ended up giving Simpson an extra blocker for his runs. By moving Seymour, Saban gave up a lot in pass receiving potential, but by now he realized the pass would not be a major factor for the Bills in 1973.

Thus, when the season opened, this was the interior line opening the holes for the Juice to flow:

At left tackle, Dave Foley, a 261-pound four-year pro out of Ohio State who had been claimed on waivers from the Jets at the start of the 1972 season. Foley, once a No. 1 draft choice, had failed in New York because of a weakness in pass blocking, a cardinal sin on any team that lists Joe Namath and his fragile knees as its primary weapon. But off his schooling at Ohio State, Foley could block for the run.

At left guard, Reggie McKenzie, coming off an outstanding rookie year. He was expected to blossom in '73.

At center, 250-pound Bruce Jarvis, a third-year pro out of Washington. Jarvis was just reaching his potential.

At right guard, Joe DeLameilleure, who quickly won the job from veteran Irv Goode.

At right tackle, Donnie Green, 272-pound third-year pro out of Purdue, a late bloomer just about ready to pop.

And at tight end, or outside tackle in the Bills' scheme of things, Paul Seymour.

Five of the six were products of the Big Ten, a muscular, running conference and one from which those pro prospects who do succeed make it in a hurry because of their background of big-time competition and coaching.

The first man off the bench was versatile Mike Montler, a fifth-year pro who had been obtained in the off-season from New England after he had demanded to be traded. Just over halfway through the year, Jarvis went down with a leg injury—in contrast to the previous season this would be the line's only casualty—and Montler took over at center with no loss in efficiency.

Adding to this picture J.D. Hill and Bob Chandler, the wide receivers, had won their jobs because they showed a talent for the crackback block. When his No. 1 fullback, Jim Braxton, showed signs of a chronic back injury, Saban moved to obtain Larry Watkins from Philadelphia in a training camp trade. Watkins proved a capable blocker and counterthreat to Simpson on runs when Braxton was unable to play.

There were two sad notes, however, as Simpson began to prepare for the new season. Al Cowlings, his closest friend on the field, was traded to Houston. Cowlings just had not produced. His departure enable O.J. and McKenzie to become roommates on the road.

More distressing, Jack Horrigan, O.J.'s closest friend off the field in Buffalo, finally succumbed that spring after a long battle against leukemia. Years earlier Horrigan had licked cancer. A man who had done that and then learned he was suffering from still another fatal disease might have been emotionally crushed. But Horrigan, though he knew the score from the beginning, continued to face each day with a smile and a wisecrack. Despite his own battle he had proved a tower of strength to Simpson during O.J.'s troubled years.

Still, the picture wasn't all glum. The Bills at last had their new stadium in suburban Orchard Park. The 80,000-seat showplace was a beauty, all the more striking because of the contrast with War Memorial Stadium. The Bills had moved from the slums to plush suburbia, from Harlem to Scarsdale, or, as O.J. could see it, from Potrero Hill to Bel Air.

Rich Stadium, its official name although the team refused to recognize this designation because they had been aced out in a bid to call it Bills Stadium, not only was a plus for games. The Bills also would practice there all week. No longer would they be forced to use makeshift facilities in bad weather. At long last Simpson and his teammates would be displayed in a big league setting. Their play would reflect the improvement.

Shortly before it became time to go to camp, Simpson talked on the phone with McKenzie. "You know, with the guys we've got to block, I think I should gain 1,700 yards this year. Maybe I'll even have a shot at Jim Brown's record," Simpson confided.

McKenzie disagreed. "Uh-uh," he whispered. "Why don't we go for the two grand?"

The seed had been planted.

Although the Bills went through their preseason schedule without a victory in six tries, Saban never lost confidence. He and his veteran players knew that the name of the preseason game is experimentation. As he put the pieces together for his 1973 edition, however, the pragmatic coach began to realize that one of them didn't quite fit. Dennis Shaw, despite his early promise, had never really progressed. What's more, his bomb-throwing style did not mesh with Saban's intended reliance on O.J. and the running game. With reluctance, Saban benched Shaw after two exhibition games and handed the quarterback job to rookie Joe Ferguson. Except for brief lapses, some forced by injury, Ferguson would handle the job the rest of the way. (Shaw ended up in complete disfavor and was traded to St. Louis after the season.)

Saban knew the risks. Pro defenses would befuddle Ferguson. Opponents would blitz on passing downs and show him an everchanging mélange of zones and man-to-man secondaries. The rookie's confidence could be forever destroyed by a flurry of interceptions. On the other hand Ferguson could be spared most of these potential horrors if Saban and his staff kept him firmly under wraps. His passing repertoire would be severely limited early in the season, and Simpson's running would buy the time as Ferguson learned to play. Any quarterback could handle an offense that consisted of Juice-left, Juice-right, and Braxton/Watkins up the middle. Shaw's problem was that he refused to do this and maybe, to tell the truth, only a rookie QB could be expected to fill such a subordinate role in what is essentially an ego position.

Ferguson was the starting quarterback when the Bills opened their season against the New England Patriots in

Foxboro, Massachusetts, but he was forced to retire in the second quarter with a concussion and Shaw took over. For once Shaw kept the ball on the ground.

The Pats scored first, missed the extra point, and then, on the first play after New England's end zone kickoff, Simpson broke outside for 80 yards and a matching touchdown. John Leypoldt kicked the extra point, and the Bills went on top for good in what developed into a 33–13 romp.

The score, however, wasn't the most significant number on this particular afternoon. Again and again, including another touchdown run of 22 yards, Simpson crashed into the line and around the Patriots' tacklers. On the sidelines late in the fourth quarter they were doing some figuring.

"Hey, man," sub receiver Ray Jarvis yelled to Simpson. "You're only 15 yards short."

Actually, Jarvis was a little off. Simpson, it turned out, was 30 yards away from the one-game record of 247 established by Willie Ellison of the Rams two years earlier.

But none of the Bills knew the correct figure at the time. Some four minutes remained in the now one-sided game, the Pats had the ball, and up and down the Buffalo bench players were yelling, "Come on, defense, get the ball back." Safety Tony Greene obliged with an interception.

With the game safely in hand, Saban hesitated to return Simpson to the lineup and risk an injury. But then he realized what a record like that could do for the Bills' esprit. They had been down so long, they needed a lift, and this could be it. Since Simpson was so close (Saban was enraged when he learned O.J. needed 30 yards, not 15), he was sent back into the fray. The Juice was weary, but the record quest put new spring in his legs.

Once again, the Bills began calling on O.J. virtually every play, and eventually he made his record with three yards to spare. After 29 carries he was relieved for the day.

As the Bills headed off the field, Reggie McKenzie shouted O.J.'s achievement for all to hear: "Two hundred and fifty yards for the Juice!"

Simpson was a few minutes late getting to the locker room because of on-field interviews, and when he arrived his teammates gave him an unprecedented standing ovation. Saban then knew that his gamble of returning O.J. to the game had been worth it.

That same afternoon Larry Watkins had run for 105 yards himself as he and Simpson set a two-man league record of 355. (O.J. also broke Cookie Gilchrist's club record of 243 yards set in 1963 against the Jets.)

"I don't think anyone will ever bad-mouth our offensive line again," Simpson proclaimed. "When two backs go over 100 yards it's a tribute to the offensive line. Our guys up front really did the job."

Simpson said he was "ecstatic" about the record "both personally and as far as the team is concerned. We both have a history of getting off to a slow start."

The Patriots were in shock.

"We were helpless. It looked like a track meet," said Chuck Fairbanks, the Pats' new coach.

"He had more yardage than Secretariat," said linebacker Edgar Chandler, a former Bill who had been traded to New England in the Mike Montler deal.

Somebody asked Patriot rookie Ray Hamilton what he thought of Simpson. The young defensive end said that he couldn't answer the question because, "I never got close enough to find out."

Films of Simpson's record game were distributed around the league as part of the regular scouting exchange. Some teams and coaches were inclined to scoff at his achievement against the lackluster Patriots. "Look at all the tackles they were missing," some sneered.

They would learn later, some the hard way, that it was O.J.'s skill, not necessarily Patriot ineptitude, that gave tacklers spaghetti arms.

The Orange Juice Express showed no signs of slowing down as Buffalo crashed through the first part of its schedule. The Bills were routed in their second game by San Diego, but Simpson still gained over 100 yards. He added 123 against the Jets, and 171 against the Eagles in close victories, but then the Baltimore Colts came to Rich Stadium, and O.J. got off to a stumbling start.

The P.A. announcer was keeping track of his progress, and O.J. discovered that thoughts of yards and records were intruding on his game concentration. Early in the second quarter, when the offense came off the field, O.J. parked himself down at the end of the bench, away from his teammates, and jammed his hands over the earholes in his helmet. For long minutes he sat there, pulling himself together as if in a trance. The game, not yards, had to be his primary focus.

With new determination O.J. trotted back on the field when the ball changed hands. He had succeeded in forcing thoughts of records and 100-yard games from his mind. He would worry only about the play at hand. The Bills won the game, 31–13, and Simpson learned that when he concentrated on the game the yards would take care of themselves. He gained 166 yards, going over 100 for the seventh straight time, including his last two outs of 1972.

Astonishingly, the Bills found themselves in a tie for first place in the AFC's Eastern Division with Miami, the defending Super Bowl champion. Both teams had 5–1 records as they met in Miami.

There, for the first time all season, O.J. was held in check. The Bills fell behind early in a 27–6 defeat, and Simpson carried only 14 times for 55 yards. On top of this he suffered a minor leg injury that kept him idle much of the second half. On the flight back he sat hunched in his seat, deep in his own thoughts. Even Reggie McKenzie knew enough to leave him be.

Talking about the Dolphins Simpson later pointed out that it was their superb defensive discipline that had done him in. What makes O.J. such an exceptional back is not just his straightaway speed or power, but the way he can change direction, cut back, and still maintain his forward momentum. Against the Dolphins he would juke (feint) the first man, but, he complained, "the other guys stayed in their lanes and were right there waiting for me." It recalled the "triangle" containment defense Notre Dame had used to keep him in check his senior year in college. It hardly soothed O.J.'s feelings when statisticians pointed out that Miami hadn't given up a 100-yard game to any runner in two seasons.

The weary Simpson had a few extra hours to rest up the following week because his next game would be a Monday nighter against the Kansas City Chiefs at home. But by this time he had become a national story, and columnists and reporters by the score were descending on Buffalo to interview him. "If I bring one more writer home, my wife will divorce me," he complained, but not too convincingly.

O.J. didn't really mind all the attention. As McKenzie perceptively pointed out, "I think he appreciates it more now because it wasn't there for a while."

Simpson had special reason for wanting to do well against the Chiefs because the game was being televised on "his" network, ABC. He really put on a show, too, as he carried 39 times for an all-time NFL record, gaining 157 yards and scoring two touchdowns in a 23–14 upset victory. During the game he went over 1,000 yards for the season, and play was halted when officials gave him the ball. Simpson went around the huddle thanking his teammates, but he really was annoyed at the ceremony. The Bills had a drive going, and he was afraid the pause would destroy their momentum. No back in NFL history had ever gone over 1,000 yards in just half a season, not even the great Jim Brown when he set all his records.

The Chiefs are one of the biggest and most physical teams in the NFL. "It was one of those real punch-out games, and I sure took my share of licks," Simpson said the next day as he soothed his battered body in the whirlpool. After only an hour in bed, O.J. had been up at dawn and was the first man at Rich Stadium when they unlocked the dressing room the next day.

"I usually have trouble getting to sleep right after a game because I'm so keyed up, but this was worse than usual," he explained. "We went out after the game and got home about 4 in the morning, but at 5 I was wide awake. I was just so sore, I knew that the sooner I got to the whirlpool the better."

O.J.'s body was paying a price for his record quest, and the mental pressure was increasing, too. The next game was a real downer as Simpson gained only 79 yards in a shocking 13–0 shutout loss to the lowly New Orleans Saints. Simpson had failed to make it on a fourth-and-one at the Saint 11, which could have turned the game early, and again he brooded all the way home. As McKenzie explained, "It wasn't the yards, man. He wouldn't mind gaining only 25 yards if the team won, but he played bad and we lost. That's what hurt."

The next week Cincinnati held O.J. one yard under 100 with a five-man line in a 16–13 victory, and then the Bills got their second shot at the Dolphins. O.J. earned personal vindication with 120 yards, but the effort was meaningless in a 17–0 defeat. This was Buffalo's third straight loss, two by shutout, and ended whatever faint hopes the Bills might have entertained of sneaking into the division championship.

Still, they did have an outside chance of making the playoffs as a wild card team. For the first time Simpson began to complain about the difficulties of gaining yardage without a passing attack to spread the defense. "It would help if we passed more," he said mildly, aware that it was a fact of life not some whim of management or coaching that kept Joe Ferguson under wraps. "It's awfully tough running against a stacked deck."

However, with four games to go, he had 1,323 yards and only one potentially difficult opponent, Atlanta. The Falcons had a rugged defense and the spur of their own wild card playoff hopes. To break Brown's record O.J. would have to average 135 yards in his remaining games.

Carrying the ball only 15 times, he fell 11 yards short of this requirement the next week in a victory over Baltimore and then came his major test against the Falcons. If they shut him off, he might be faced with an insurmountable task in his final two games against New England and New York.

If he needed further incentive, though, he got it from sharp-tongued, short-tempered Norm Van Brocklin, the Atlanta coach. Van Brocklin earlier had said of Simpson, "He never could play for me because he won't put his nose in there. He doesn't like contact."

"If he means he doesn't like it because I'd rather run away from a tackler than over him, I guess then I'll never play for Van Brocklin," Simpson countered with a flicker of a smile. But the insinuation that he lacked courage still rankled.

Simpson's running style actually had undergone several drastic changes during his football career.

Back when he was in junior college and just starting at Southern Cal, he often bragged how he liked to put the wood to would-be tacklers so they would have bruises to remember him with next time he came their way.

"I run to hit the tackler before he hits me," O.J. told Dan Jenkins of *Sports Illustrated* early in his Trojan career. "I want to be the punisher, not him."

However, as time passed O.J. realized he no longer was bigger than most of the people he played against. He developed the cut-back style of running, which proved so effective in college.

This was a technique he carried over to pro ball, but the stutter-step action behind the line of scrimmage wasn't nearly as effective in the NFL.

As Simpson headed into what would be his record year, close observers of his career noticed still another striking change in style. The stutter-step had been discarded. For the first time he was slamming into the holes with what coaches like to call "reckless abandon."

Simpson had a simple explanation for the change. "In the old days, with the offensive line we used to have in Buffalo, I never could be sure the hole would be where it was supposed to be. So I'd kind of dance around waiting to see where something would open up. This year, with the cats I've got blocking, I *know* the hole will be there."

Still, Simpson continued to insist it was wise to run away from tacklers if possible. "I don't believe in putting my head down and running over guys," he said one day. "If I have to for one yard, for a first down or a touchdown, I'll try, but I don't believe that when I step out on the field I have to prove how much of a man I am, showing I'm tougher than the other guys. My first few years I went out of bounds a lot of times and didn't feel nothin' about it, in spite of what Van Brocklin says. I admire Larry Brown [Washington's 195-pounder who likes to pretend he's Larry Csonka] for his courage, but beat up is all it got him. And I've told him if he keeps it up he's going to end up punchy. Challenging tacklers takes its toll.

"Sure I like to get paid, but I still play the game for fun most of all. I still want to play the game the way I did in the playground and rather than tell how I ran over four guys in San Francisco one day, I'd rather tease guys I know about how I juked them."

"Yeah, Juice," Robert James interrupted Simpson one time, "I saw you putting that old okey-dokey on some people out there, but you know you couldn't do that to me."

To which Simpson replied with an indulgent smile, "Just don't get traded, Robert."

Simpson also likes to point out that his teammates often will insist that coaches stop the projector and rerun the film anytime they see O.J. throwing a block. But while making light of his fondness for contact, Juice also brags that "90 percent of the time when somebody intercepts a pass against us, I'm the one who makes the tackle." He's proud that he first made his junior college rep on defense, and nobody can deny that he makes most of his yardage inside the tackles where contact is part of the play.

Generally, Simpson avoids those disabling heavy shots. "You don't see good backs get blind-sided," he has said, and coaches marvel how he seems to sense tacklers around him. Part is peripheral vision, part instinct, the same combination that has kept scrambling quarterback Fran Tarkenton alive all these years.

Despite Buffalo's cold weather, O.J. prefers short-sleeved jerseys. "I can feel tacklers better that way," he says. "I can feel their touch, and in a football game I just don't want to be touched."

This instinct rather than power enables him to break so many tackles. He can change direction or accelerate before the tackler gets a good grip on him.

Van Brocklin might have been pondering all this as he steamed on the sidelines while Simpson, the man who couldn't play for him, shredded his proud defense for 137 yards in a 17–6 Buffalo victory that ended Atlanta's play-off hopes.

During this late run at the record, Jim Braxton, recovered from his sore back, had returned to the starting lineup. He was more of a rushing threat than Watkins, and his counter plays took some of the pressure off Simpson. At the same time Saban began to let Ferguson throw a little more, which helped, too.

Still, as he came into his final two games, O.J. needed 280 yards to break Brown's record.

The New England Patriots provided Buffalo's final home opposition in the next-to-last game of the season. The date was December 9, a long way from Buffalo's "other season," the Fourth of July. The Rich Stadium Astroturf was frozen solid. The gods protecting Jim Brown's record would not make it easy for O.J.

Simpson, however, was not concerned. He felt he had developed a technique for running on a frozen field. It was similar to the method he used on a slippery artificial turf, such as often was found in Miami.

"You don't let your feet really leave the ground, you sort of glide along," he explained.

The year before he had enjoyed a big game on a frozen field late in the season in Buffalo, and afterward he had gone out with several teammates to celebrate the victory. As they headed home on somewhat unsteady feet, the other players cautioned O.J. to watch his step.

"Don't worry," he replied airily, "didn't I just prove today that I can walk on i-i-i-i-c-c-c-e!"

Relating the tale of his flop on the ice, O.J. roars with laughter.

As he pulled on his uniform to face the Patriots, he knew he would be steady on his feet, no matter what the weather conditions. It was snowing at game time, huge wet flakes, but neither O.J. nor the Rich Stadium fans—by now O.J. was calling them the best in football—were discouraged.

While all the other players were slipping and sliding, Simpson kept his feet for 22 carries that netted 219 yards in a 37–13 rout. Considering the weather conditions and the defensive pressure, this was an even greater performance than his opening 250 yards against the same team.

O.J.'s second 200-yard performance of the season, equaling another Jim Brown mark, left him only 60 yards short of the coveted record. He knew he would make that with ease in his final game the next week in New York. Only one real challenge remained. Reggie McKenzie had posed it for him many months before when he whispered, "Why don't we go for the two grand?"

12

"What Do You Want Me to Do?"

The 1974 Pro Bowl was threatening to turn into a fiasco. Thousands of tickets already had been sold for the late January game in Kansas City's Arrowhead Stadium, but record cold and heavy snows gave the area an arctic air two weeks before the game. Worse was threatened. The weather was so bad, it made even Buffalo look good.

There was no question of moving the game because the stadium was almost sold out. But finally NFL Commissioner Pete Rozelle was forced to order the competing players to report to San Diego instead of Kansas City for their week-long practice sessions. Two days before the Pro Bowl, the ensemble would move *en masse* to Kansas City.

All this, of course, turned the game into a promotional nightmare, but worse was yet to come. As the All-Stars convened for practice, one notable figure was missing. O.J. Simpson, the biggest name in pro football, was nowhere to be found.

This certainly was not like O.J., a man who always lives up to his obligations. But when he finally was contacted after dozens of phone calls, it turned out the Juice was acting strictly in character after all. Early in the season he had been discussing the Pro Bowl and the lack of recognition being given Buffalo's offensive line. On that occasion he made a public vow to sportswriter Jim Baker: "I won't play in it this year if someone from our offensive line isn't chosen with me."

When the 1974 Pro Bowl squads were made public, not one Buffalo lineman was included. The Juice was boiling. (He also was misinformed. He thought the squad was put together arbitrarily. Rather, it is chosen strictly by vote of coaches in each conference who are not allowed to name their own players.) With his disappearing act Simpson was merely making good on his earlier promise.

"I know now it was the wrong thing to do," he apologized when informed of how the squad was chosen. "But I did make a promise, and that's the way it has to be."

Fortunately, although that particular Miami lineman may not agree, Dolphin tackle Wayne Moore had played through the Super Bowl with a bad leg. At the last minute he was excused from his Pro Bowl obligation, and Buffalo's Dave Foley was named to replace him. Trained always to follow his blockers, O.J. reported docilely to camp.

Simpson had facts to support his esteem for the linemen who wore Buffalo red, white, and blue that year. And it went beyond his personal record of 2,003 yards. As a team the Bills had gained 3,088 yards rushing, which was more than any pro club had ever gained in the 54-year history of the NFL. The old record of 2,960 had been established the year before by the undefeated Miami world champions with a balanced offense that included a dangerous passing attack and two certified 1,000-yard rushers in Larry Csonka and Mercury Morris. "We gained over 3,000 yards with a rookie quarterback and two rookie linemen, that's why I feel our offensive line didn't get the recognition it deserved," O.J. pointed out.

All winter the rewards flowed in for Simpson, including the prestigious Hickok Belt as Pro Athlete of the Year. At every appearance Simpson lauded his teammates, and, if asked, he indicated he might do even better the next season if the Bills would throw the ball more. A 3,000-yard season was not out of reach, he said.

To Simpson, his record year meant many things.

First, of course, there was recognition as one of the best running backs ever to play the game.

"When I was in college and during my first three years in Buffalo, the toughest thing was to read about other running backs and the honors they were receiving," Simpson related frankly. "I knew I was as good as they were, but nobody else did because I never had the chance to prove it. But now I feel I've done my thing, and I'm satisfied with myself. And the people know what I can do, too. I would go to All-Star games [as a spectator], and I would be angry because I felt I could do as well as those guys. Now I don't *think* I can do as well as those guys, I *know* I can do as well . . . and the people know it, too.

"When I left college I was glad to know people thought of me as the best because of the Heisman Trophy. That's why I'm glad to break these records, because Jim Brown was considered the best."

The revival of the Bills' franchise also provided intense satisfaction for O.J. It doesn't mean much to break records with a loser, and in 1973 the Bills reversed their fortunes with an eminently respectable 9–5 record. They retained an outside chance of making the playoffs until the final West Coast scores came in on the last Sunday of the season.

"Being in Buffalo during those lean years, it was anguish," Simpson recalled. "We played on God forsaken War Memorial Stadium, I didn't get along with the coach, and I wasn't being used the way you'd expect them to use a No. 1 draft choice.

"Worse, our team was the laughingstock of pro football . . . and played like it. The organization didn't seem to be *trying* to win football games as we went from four victories to three to one in three years. But today we're a first-rate organization playing in a brand new stadium, and I think we're only one or two players and one year in experience from being a real championship contender.

"It's a very satisfying feeling," Simpson continued solemnly. "You know, I never asked to be traded. I figured I belonged to Buffalo, and this was where I would play. I guess I could have been traded to Miami or some other contender, and it would have been fun playing there, but I never would have had the same sense of accomplishment, the feeling that I helped build something, the way I do right now with the Buffalo Bills."

All the trophies and plaques and inner satisfactions are nice, but they won't help buy Arnella and Jason a new pair of shoes. O.J. also reaped financial benefits from his emergence as a running star.

Along with everything else representing Buffalo, Ralph Wilson also wasn't one of O.J.'s favorites during those early years. It all stemmed from their initial contract negotiations. Simpson resented the way Wilson had broken their compact not to divulge details of their talks, and he felt personally demeaned by what he felt were the owner's efforts to paint him as a greedy punk kid. He did not appreciate Wilson's hardline attitude.

"During those negotiations he told me he would pay me more than the others getting out of college, because I did more than anyone else in college, but he couldn't see paying me what I wanted because I hadn't done anything in pro ball. I thought this was a whole bunch of hullaballo," says Simpson who, honestly, seldom uses profanity.

During his first three seasons Simpson did little to warrant an upward adjustment in his contract, and there were many who felt he deserved a cut. Simpson's request for a renewal at the start of his fourth training camp was well received by management, but this could have been taken as the price Wilson was willing to pay to smooth the path for his new coach.

Later that year, however, Wilson made good on his pledge to reward O.J. when the Juice started "doing something" in pro ball. During the 1972 campaign, as he was heading toward his first 1,000-yard season, Simpson received from his boss a voluntary upward adjustment in salary.

Then, after four games of the 1973 season, Wilson called him in again, offering not only still another raise but a five-year extension of his contract that O.J. says, "ties me up with the Buffalo Bills for the rest of my pro career."

Today, Simpson's admiration for Wilson as an owner and an honorable man is open and boundless. "When he challenged me to produce as a pro, I thought he was just putting me off and putting me down, but now I realize it was simply part of his business philosophy," Simpson said. "The minute I started producing in pro ball, I didn't have to go to him, he was right there. You can't ask more from a man."

Simpson, of course, has meant more to the Bills and Buffalo than just a stud who can gain 2,000 yards on command. If that were the case he would rate no more recognition than Secretariat, the Triple Crown-winning thoroughbred.

"O.J. is a strong motivating force on this team," says Saban. "He helps bring the team together in creating what you could call a community atmosphere. He does it all [in practice], and so the others can't complain. O.J. carries a great load on his shoulders, and I'm trying to spread it out now because you can't have a great football team with one man carrying all the responsibility. But it was O.J. who bought us the time, gave us the chance to get out from under."

Saban pointed out that only 10 men who had been in his first Buffalo camp two years earlier had survived to witness O.J.'s record-setting game against the Jets. Simpson and Robert James were the only ones left from the squad they had greeted as rookies in 1969.

Off the field, too, Simpson has been an important force in the Buffalo community. He underscored his new sense of belonging before the 1973 season when he and Marguerite for the first time bought furniture and set up housekeeping in a rented Buffalo townhouse complex. (Reggie McKenzie lived across the courtyard.) True, they hotfooted it back to California when the season ended, but the purchase of furniture seemed to give them a few more roots than previous seasons when they rented a furnished apartment. Buffalo citizens also noted that Simpson remained in his "old" neighborhood, not far from downtown, instead of moving to a distant suburb near the new stadium, as did many of his teammates.

Bob Lustig, basically Wilson's overseer of the Bills, probably knows O.J. off the field better than any member of the current organization. "Each year, you could see O.J. getting more and more involved in the community, which is important, because the people here are rather sensitive to their reputation as the butt of jokes," the former Detroiter has pointed out.

"I remember on the plane ride back from Atlanta, Juice commented to one of the writers that he thought it would be a good idea to mention in the paper what great fans we have in Buffalo. He wanted to point out that we had a chance (since realized) to lead the NFL in actual attendance this year. Miami would sell more tickets, but they were leading the league in no-shows, too. He was very proud of our attendance, and I think it helped community pride to realize the city could be No. 1 in something. It was O.J. who pointed it out."

Like many urban centers Buffalo has a large black population, and most civic leaders agree that O.J.'s presence has helped ease potential racial tensions. "As a black star, he is a good bridge to the community, especially when someone is as free with his time and as understanding as O.J. is," Lustig notes.

Buffalo is not completely a wasteland, but until O.J. Simpson showed up and became a star, about the last local resident citizens could brag on was Millard Fillmore, a one-term president back before the Civil War.

O.J.'s off-field presence is seen in many areas in Buffalo. He remains constantly on call for civic appearances, generally where children are involved, and after the bloody Attica Prison uprising in Upstate New York, he helped organize a group of players to visit the scene. Just by talking football to the inmates, they helped restore some sense of normality to the prison . . . and also showed that someone outside cared.

The other touches are effective, if not so dramatic, ranging from a smile and a "How're ya' doing?" to fans in a neighborhood pub to the sight of the great O.J. Simpson stopping his car on the way home from practice to get involved with a local high school team working out in a playground.

"I could see O.J. change over the years," Lustig continues. "I could see him involving himself with the team, recognizing what business distractions could cause. He had to recognize and get first things first in proper order, but now he has become a thoroughly professional ballplayer."

How long will Simpson remain a professional ballplayer?"

O.J. does not see his career as open-ended, grinding to a lackluster halt only after he's been seriously injured or when he can no longer put one arthritic knee in front of the other.

"When I got out of college, football was everything to me, but now I can see myself sitting up there as a spectator enjoying the games," he says.

The dominant figure that influences Simpson's thinking is that of Jim Brown, and not just because they wore the same number, played the same position, and eventually may end up in the same profession, acting.

Brown is an important symbol to all black athletes because he was able to look the white establishment straight in the eye, succeed in their environment on his own terms, and then, without a backward, glance walk away into another lucrative and visible career. That he was able to walk away with his body still unscarred by injury makes him an awesome figure to all athletes no matter what their color.

Jim Brown played only nine professional seasons. He was all set to play a tenth in 1966 when shooting was delayed that summer on a movie in which he was appearing, *The Dirty Dozen.* Forced by circumstance to choose right then between completing the picture or reporting on time to training camp, Brown summarily announced his retirement from football. In only nine seasons he had gained a league record 12,312 yards, almost 4,000 more yards than the next man in line. (After five seasons O.J.'s career total is 5,181.)

Simpson considers himself "more elusive" but feels Brown was "more physically gifted" as a runner because of his strength.

The two are direct opposites in personality as well as

running style. Whereas O.J. is gregarious and bubbly, happy with himself, Brown was sullen and withdrawn, barely concealing his hostilities. Ernie Kellerman, a late pickup for the Bills' secondary in 1973, also played with Brown in Cleveland. He rates O.J. much higher as a team leader. When he joined the Bills at midseason, Kellerman recalls how Simpson came over and introduced himself, a gesture the veteran safety would not have expected from Brown. Brown was a member of the team only on the field.

Within the pro football family there is no question that O.J. was better liked. (Brown even referred to this mutual hostility on the occasion of his induction into the Hall of Fame, but it also didn't keep him from being elected the first year he was eligible.) That's why so many people in football were pulling for Simpson to break Brown's records.

Brown and Simpson both live in Los Angeles and are friends, of sorts. They run in some of the same show business circles, although their life-styles differ, and occasionally meet in pickup basketball games at Brown's home. "We don't talk business," O.J. says, business meaning football. And all through his record year, including the finale, Simpson never once heard from Brown. "But that's nothing," he tossed off lightly. "I never heard from him before, either."

Early in 1973 Simpson disclosed four personal goals he had set for himself in pro football. He achieved one, gaining over 2,000 yards in one season. Another goal is to gain 300 yards in one game, as he did in junior college. The fourth depends on the third. He wants to get Buffalo into a Super Bowl and, at that point, retire on top. Significantly, he did not anticipate staying around long enough to break Brown's career record.

"I may admire Jim Brown more because he made the decision to quit while he was on top than for his physical ability," O.J. says. "Maybe that's why he's able to play those movie roles as supercat, wiping out the Mafia and stuff, because people last remember him as a superplayer. When you think of Johnny Unitas today, it's not as the superplayer he once was, but as the guy everybody thinks should have quit.

"If I retired, though, without the Bills ever making it to the Super Bowl, it would always be a claw in my chest," Simpson continues. But he points out, "Even now I'm thinking of other things to do . . . and I'm almost ready to do them."

Retirement from sports, O.J. vows, will not be for him the traumatic experience that it has been for other athletes.

"Just the thought of going into a restaurant and having to wait for a table, it frightens us," Simpson admitted one day between takes in the cavernous ABC television studios on New York's West Side. "Leaving sports, you have that fear of never having done anything else. I'm trying to avoid that fear. I can understand why so many players get divorces a year or two after they quit. The only thing I can compare it to is a woman's menopause. You're losing something that's very important to you."

Thus, from his days at Southern Cal when he worked summers in the movie studios, Simpson has dedicated himself to preparing for a career in the entertainment field. "And I don't want to be just an expert analyst on football and track," he insists.

Simpson points out that sports and acting are compatible.

"Take a guy like Joe [Namath] or me, acting is the only thing we can get into to get the same ego trip," he said. "Athletes are people who set out to do something and *do* it right now. Every week in football I get to feed that ego, and I'm doing it with *me,* not with a machine or something. Well, your job as an actor is projecting *you,* getting *you* across. Some of the most confident people in the world —and it comes off as cockiness sometimes—are athletes, and that's because they know what they can do."

Simpson has had dramatic roles in several television shows, and after his record season was given a supporting part in the movie *The Klansman.* He has turned down more important roles.

"I'm declining now to get into a role where I'm a featured guy, because I'm not yet that good an actor," he explained frankly. "If I go into acting, I want to be a good one, and the important thing now is to work with good actors. I don't want to jump right in to exploit my name, the way a lot of athletes have done."

Simpson thus is following the same path as Jim Brown, who also was handled carefully during his early years as a performer until he was deemed ready to handle a major rôle. (Most critics believe O.J.'s future is even brighter than Brown's because he has a less inhibited personality. Brown's acting range, even now, is limited.)

If he sticks to this resolve Simpson will avoid the mistakes of his friend, Joe Namath. After the Jets and Namath won the Super Bowl, the young quarterback had a chance to make movies a full-time career. Sonny Werblin, one of the great talent agents before he got into sports, had just been forced out as president of the Jets by his partners. As a favor to Joe, whom he had signed out of college, Werblin offered to handle Namath's career. His plan was to place Joe in top properties and slowly bring him along, as had been done with Brown. Namath, instead, listened to other voices. He snubbed Werblin and allowed himself to be thrown in over his head into featured roles in three extremely forgettable movies. Years later he and his advisers were still trying to salvage Joe's movie career from the wreckage.

After his record season Simpson resumed his association with ABC as anchorman for the network's Sunday afternoon series of sports shows. "I call it on-the-job training, and I feel fortunate to get it," he says.

Simpson's first contact with ABC's innovative sports chief, Roone Arledge, came his junior year in college. They met at a dinner in Detroit. "He impressed me then as we talked, and he told me he wanted to learn the business and had taken some courses along those lines at Southern Cal," Arledge recalls. "He struck me as willing to work and anxious to learn."

A year later at the Heisman Trophy dinner in New York, the two men met again and nailed down a flexible long-term arrangement dependant on Simpson's availability.

"We're still looking for ways to use him," says Arledge, who predicts that Simpson eventually "will be a major motion picture personality."

One of the men in Simpson's corner is Howard Cosell,

the oft-abrasive ABC sportscaster who has taken an almost parental interest in O.J.'s career.

"He has natural presence and charm," says Cosell, "and it shines right through. He'll be a great performer, far and above any role as a sports announcer."

Cosell and Simpson have been friends since O.J.'s college days. One night Howard took the Heisman Trophy winner down to Bachelors III, the controversial New York bar Namath then was being ordered to sell by Commissioner Rozelle.

They got there ahead of Namath and when Joe walked in, Cosell impatiently wanted to call him over. "Uh-uh, Howard," Simpson cautioned. "You don't rush the great ones." And so he let Namath set the stage for their meeting.

Cosell and Simpson continue a bandying relationship. "You need a rehearsal?" producer John Martin called over to Simpson before one particularly tricky Sunday bit. "Naaah," O.J. yelled back, making sure Cosell and his ego both were listening. "I don't need a rehearsal, I've been around Howard all day."

And when Cosell asked Simpson, who was playing a noisy game of gin with the stagehands, if he was worried about choking up on a segment they had to do together, O.J. replied with a chuckle, "Don't worry, Howard, the best brings out the best."

Simpson is not above getting professional instruction to improve his natural talents, the same way he went to a pro to polish his backhand after he'd taught himself tennis. Only in this field it's diction lessons.

He also has to discipline himself to stand still when he's

on camera because "usually when I'm workin' I'm movin'."

Simpson feels he came along at just the right time. "I arrived when black became vogue," he says. "Every studio in California and all the major companies in the United States were putting out those memorandums, 'Hire more blacks,' and I was right there. Remember, there were no blacks in the endorsement field until I signed with Chevrolet. I was in the right place at the right time. Now I think America has arrived to the point where people who deserve it get it."

Simpson, however, sees more in his future than the various ways he can earn a living.

"When I was in college, I thought that when I finished with football I would work full-time with kids in the ghetto," he says, "but now I realize that this would be impossible. My ego just wouldn't let me go back to the playgrounds."

But this doesn't mean Simpson has turned his back on his past. He insists he will seek other ways to pay off his debt to the people who helped him.

He knows that as a professional football player, his free time is limited. After a few more years in the game, though, he will have the financial independence to work for youth causes without worrying "What's it going to cost me?" He knows a football career is short and that he must make it financially when he can.

The organization that most interests Simpson is called Direction Sports, founded in Los Angeles by a man named Tulley Brown. Brown believes that sports can be linked to academic achievement for underprivileged kids. A youngster may have to answer an "academic" question before he's allowed to bat in a baseball game, for instance. (Medicine, movies, mechanics, and other fields also are linked to the program.)

Simpson notes proudly that the Direction Sports motto —"My Hero, the Pimp"—was adopted by Tulley Brown from something O.J. pointed out in one of their early conversations. It stemmed from Simpson's recollection of his own youth and from the profound influence on his life of that long-ago exposure to the affluence of Willie Mays.

"I told Tulley that it was so easy for kids to get misdirected in the ghetto, because the only guys they saw who were dressed well and drove big cars were the pimps," O.J. explained. "In my neighborhood in San Francisco, they were the ones with the diamond rings and flashy cars. When you're a kid, you want all those things, too, so your hero is the pimp who's standing right there. What I tried to tell Tulley was that you've got to furnish those kids with alternative heroes.

"My involvement in this is not as much as I once planned or as much as I would really like, but being a professional ball player your career is only so long. As I told Tulley, if I ended up as a playground director, I would not be setting an example. I used to meet guys at the playground who were former ballplayers and stuff, and it was good having them there . . . but this was not what I wanted to be. I could only listen to them so far, because if going to school and studying and all that just got me right back here on the playground, that was not what I wanted. That pimp is still driving an El Dorado, and that playground director is still driving a Volkswagen and material things are still important to the youth.

"So that's the way I look at it. You only play football so long and the [business] opportunities only present themselves so long, and I've got to get as much as I can now in order to set the kind of example I want to set.

"People say that when you're hot is when they need you the most, and I agree. That's why I do what I do now. But I've always wanted to have a program where I could do what I wanted to do [for kids] and spend the time on it that I want to spend and not have to worry about what it's going to cost me and not have to worry about whether I'm putting enough money away for my own daughter and son to go to college. That's why I talk about playing only a few more years, because then I'll be financially solvent."

When he looks back at his own childhood, Simpson is not that unhappy about it. "I had a ball, and I wouldn't change a thing," he says. "I never did anything more than the other kids in my environment." O.J. understands the stealing and the fights and everything else involved in survival in the ghetto. He still cannot bring himself to condemn out of hand the ghetto kids who do the things he did because he knows what drives them to it. (A blunt statement that he didn't think these things were that "wrong," repeated on a radio station, once triggered a flood of reproving phone calls.) But Simpson knows that a society that does not want a young man to steal should provide him other avenues for his energy and ambition . . . and food for his family's table, too.

His friend Joe Bell took the big fall and climbed back, and O.J. knows how close he, too, came to disaster. He appreciates his escape.

"Everything that's happened to me, it's so unreal at times," he confessed one day during his glory year. "I've got everything I wanted, and, when I get to the Super Bowl, I'll say: 'Hey, what else can I ask for?' "

Then O.J. paused, and his laughing eyes turned serious. "And I'll also ask, 'What do You want me to do?' "

Record Section

O.J. Simpson's Records with the Buffalo Bills

Career Rushing Totals

Games	No.	Yds.	Avg.	TDs.
63	1108	5,181	4.67	30

Additional Career Totals

Receiving	94	911	9.6	3
Kickoff Returns	33	991	30.0	0
Passing	6–14	110	18.3	1

Rushing Statistics—Home & Away

	Games	Avg.	No.	Yds.	TDs.
HOME	32	576	2,571	4.46	17
AWAY	31	532	2,610	4.90	13

Summary—High/Low Rushing Marks

Single Game:
- Most Carries—39 vs. Kansas City (10/29/73)
- Most Yards—250 vs. New England (9/16/73)
- Highest Avg.—9.1 (82 yds. on 9 carries) vs. Miami (9/26/71)

Most TDs.–2 vs. New England (9/16/73), Baltimore (10/14/73), Kansas City (10/29/73)
Fewest Carries–6 vs. Oakland (10/19/69)
Fewest Yards–Minus 10 vs. Baltimore (10/10/71)
Lowest Avg.–0.00 vs. Baltimore (10/10/71)

Single Season:
Most Carries–332 (1973)
Most Yards–2,003 (1973)
Highest Avg.–6.03 (1973)
Most TDs.–12 (1973)
Fewest Yards–488 (1970)
Fewest Yards–488 1970
Lowest Avg.–3.9 (1969)
Fewest TDs.–2 (1969)

Vs. Single Opponent (Career):
Most Carries–184 vs. N.Y. Jets (10 games)
Most Yards–946 vs. New England (8 games)
Highest Avg.–6.9 vs. Pittsburgh (2 games)
Most TDs.–7 vs. New England (8 games)

NFL Records Set by O.J. Simpson in 1973

Most yards in one season–2,003 (breaks old record of 1,863 set by Jim Brown of the Cleveland Browns in 1963).

Most carries in one season–332 (breaks old record of 305 set by Jim Brown in 1961 when he gained 1,408 yards).

Most games 100 yards or more in one season–11 (breaks old record of nine set by Jim Brown in 1963).

Most games 200 yards or more in one season–3 (breaks old record of two set by Jim Brown in 1963).

Most yards in one game–250 against New England September 16 (breaks old record of 247 set by Willie Ellison of the Los Angeles Rams against New Orleans December 5, 1971).

Most carries in one game–39 against Kansas City October 29 (breaks old record of 38 set by Harry Newman of the New York Giants against Green Bay Packers November 11, 1934, and equaled by Jim Nance of the Boston Patriots against Oakland Raiders October 30, 1966).

(Buffalo Bills as a team set a record with 3,088 yards rushing for the season, breaking old record of 2,960 set by the Miami Dolphins in 1972).

O.J. vs. the NFL

	GAMES	CARRIES	YDS.	AVG.	TD
Atlanta	1	24	137	5.7	0
Baltimore	6	88	410	4.2	4
Chicago	No games				
Cincinnati	3	43	174	4.0	2
Cleveland	1	27	93	3.4	1
Dallas	1	14	25	1.8	1
Denver	2	42	162	3.9	1
Detroit	1	27	116	4.3	0
Green Bay	No games				
Houston	3	44	114	2.6	1
Kansas City	4	80	328	4.1	3
Los Angeles	1	14	24	1.7	0
Miami	9	124	568	4.6	1
Minnesota	1	12	45	3.8	0
N.Y. Giants	No games				
N.Y. Jets	10	184	829	4.5	4
New England	8	150	946	6.3	7
New Orleans	1	20	79	3.9	0
Oakland	2	34	194	5.7	0
Philadelphia	1	27	171	6.3	1
Pittsburgh	2	36	249	6.9	2
San Diego	3	47	236	5.0	1
San Francisco	1	29	138	4.8	0
St. Louis	1	16	42	2.6	0
Washington	1	26	101	3.9	1
TOTALS	63	1108	5,181	4.67	30

100 Yard Games

DATE	OPPONENT	CARRIES	YDS.	AVG.	TD
9/29/69	Denver	24	110	4.6	0
11/1/70	@Boston	17	123	7.2	1
10/23/71	@ San Diego	18	106	5.9	0
9/24/71	San Francisco	29	138	4.8	0
10/15/72	@Oakland	28	144	5.1	0
10/29/72	Pittsburgh	22	189	8.6	1
11/19/72	@New England	22	103	4.7	1
12/10/72	Detroit	27	116	4.3	0
12/17/72	@Washington	26	101	3.9	1
9/16/73	@New England	29	250	8.6	2
9/23/73	@San Diego	22	103	4.7	1
9/30/73	New York Jets	24	123	5.1	0
10/7/73	Philadelphia	27	171	6.3	1
10/14/73	Baltimore	22	166	7.5	2
10/29/73	Kansas City	39	157	4.0	2
11/18/73	Miami	20	120	6.0	0
11/25/73	@Baltimore	15	124	8.3	1
12/2/73	@Atlanta	24	137	5.7	0
12/9/73	New England	22	219	10.0	1
12/16/73	@New York Jets	34	200	5.9	1

1973 Season

DATE	OPPONENT	CARRIES	YDS.	AVG.	TD
9/16	@New England Patriots	29	250	8.6	2
9/23	@San Diego Chargers	22	103	4.7	1
9/30	New York Jets	24	123	5.1	0
10/7	Philadelphia Eagles	27	171	6.3	1
10/14	Baltimore Colts	22	166	7.5	2
10/21	@Miami Dolphins	14	55	3.9	0
10/29	Kansas City Chiefs	39	157	4.0	2
11/4	@New Orleans Saint	20	79	3.9	0
11/10	Cincinnati Bengals	20	99	4.9	1
11/18	Miami Dolphins	20	120	6.0	0
11/25	@Baltimore Colts	15	124	8.3	1
12/2	@Atlanta Falcons	24	137	5.7	0
12/9	New England	22	219	10.0	1
12/16	@New York Jets	34	200	5.9	1
	Totals	332	2,003	6.03	12

1972 Season

DATE	OPPONENT	CARRIES	YDS.	AVG.	TD
9/17/72	New York Jets	14	41	2.9	0
9/24/72	San Francisco 49ers	29	138	4.8	0
10/1/72	Baltimore Colts	21	78	3.7	0
10/8/72	New England Patriots	13	31	2.4	1
10/15/72	@Oakland Raiders	28	144	5.1	0
10/22/72	@Miami Dolphins	16	57	3.6	0
10/29/72	Pittsburgh Steelers	22	189	8.6	1
11/5/72	Miami Dolphins	13	45	3.5	0
11/12/72	@New York Jets	20	89	4.5	0
11/19/72	@New England Patriots	22	103	4.7	1
11/26/72	@Cleveland Browns	27	93	3.4	1
12/3/72	@Baltimore Colts	14	26	1.9	1
12/10/72	Detroit Lions	27	116	4.3	0
12/17/72	@Washington Redskins	26	101	3.9	1
	Totals	292	1251	4.3	6

1971 Season

DATE	OPPONENT	CARRIES	YDS.	AVG.	TD
9/19/71	Dallas Cowboys	14	25	1.8	1
9/26/71	Miami Dolphins	9	82	9.1	1
10/13/71	@Minnesota Vikings	12	45	3.8	0
10/10/71	Baltimore Colts	7	—10	—	0
10/17/71	@New York Jets	18	69	3.8	1
10/23/71	@San Diego Chargers	18	106	5.9	0
10/31/71	St. Louis Cardinals	16	42	2.6	0
11/7/71	@Miami Dolphins	10	90	9.0	0
11/14/71	@New England Patriots	16	61	3.8	0
11/21/71	New York Jets	14	48	3.4	0
11/28/71	New England Patriots	14	61	4.4	1
12/5/71	@Baltimore Colts	9	26	2.9	0
12/12/71	Houston Oilers	12	29	2.4	1
12/19/71	@Kansas City Chiefs	14	68	4.9	0
	Totals	183	742	4.1	5

1970 Season

DATE	OPPONENT	CARRIES	YDS.	AVG.	TD
9/20/70	Denver Broncos	18	52	2.9	1
9/27/70	Los Angeles Rams	14	24	1.7	0
10/4/70	New York Jets	21	99	4.7	1
10/11/70	@Pittsburgh Steelers	14	60	4.3	1
10/18/70	Miami Dolphins	11	35	3.2	0
10/25/70	@New York Jets	15	55	3.7	0
11/1/70	@Boston Patriots	17	123	7.2	1
11/8/70	Cinn. Bengals	10	40	4.0	1
11/15/70	@Baltimore Colts		Did not play		
11/22/70	@Chicago Bears		Did not play		
11/29/70	Boston Patriots		Did not play		
12/6/70	@New York Giants		Did not play		
12/13/70	Baltimore Colts		Did not play		
12/20/70	@Miami Dolphins		Did not play		
	Totals	120	488	4.1	5

1969 Season

DATE	OPPONENT	CARRIES	YDS.	AVG.	TD
9/14/69	New York Jets	10	35	3.5	1
9/21/69	Houston Oilers	19	58	3.1	0
9/28/69	Denver Broncos	24	110	4.6	0
10/5/69	@Houston Oilers	13	27	2.1	0
10/11/69	Boston Patriots		Did not play		
10/19/69	@Oakland Raiders	6	50	8.3	0
10/26/69	@Miami Dolphins	10	12	1.2	0
11/2/69	Kansas City Chiefs	16	41	2.6	0
11/9/69	@New York Jets	14	70	5.0	0
11/16/69	Miami Dolphins	21	72	3.4	0
11/23/69	@Boston Patriots	17	98	5.8	0
11/30/69	Cinn. Bengals	13	35	2.7	0
12/7/69	@Kansas City Chiefs	11	62	5.6	1
12/14/69	@San Diego Chargers	7	27	3.9	0
	Totals	181	697	3.9	2

University of Southern California

1967 Season

GAME	TCB	RUSHING NET	AVG.	TD	PA	PASSING PC	YDS.	TD	REC.	RECEIVING YDS.	AVG.
Washington State	17	94	5.5	1	0	0	0	0	2	28	14.00
Texas	30	158	5.3	1	0	0	0	0	1	20	20.00
Michigan State	36	190	5.2	2	1	1	7	1	1	2	2.00
Stanford	29	160	5.5	0	2	1	9	1	2	52	26.00
Notre Dame	38	150	3.9	3	0	0	0	0	1	—2	—2.00
Washington	30	235	7.8	2	2	1	17	1	0	0	0.00
Oregon	23	63	2.7	0	0	0	0	0	1	9	9.00
California		did not play									
Oregon State	33	188	5.7	0	0	0	0	0	2	0	0.00
UCLA	30	177	5.9	2	0	0	0	0	0	0	0.00
*Indiana	25	128	5.1	2	1	0	0	0	0	0	0.00
TOTALS	291	1543	5.3	13	6	3	33	3	10	109	10.90

1968 Season

GAME	TCB	RUSHING NET	AVG.	TD	PA	PASSING PC	YDS.	TD	REC.	RECEIVING YDS.	AVG.
Minnesota	39	236	6.05	4	1	0	0	0	6	57	9.50
Northwestern	34	189	5.56	3	0	0	0	0	0	0	0.00
Miami	38	163	4.28	2	1	0	0	0	2	10	5.00
Stanford	47	220	4.68	3	1	1	15	0	1	4	4.00
Washington	33	172	5.21	2	0	0	0	0	0	0	0.00
Oregon	25	67	2.68	1	0	0	0	0	1	—4	—4.00
California	31	164	5.30	2	0	0	0	0	0	0	0.00
Oregon State	47	238	5.07	1	0	0	0	0	2	12	6.00
UCLA	40	205	5.12	3	0	0	0	0	3	24	8.00
Notre Dame	21	55	2.62	1	0	0	0	0	3	23	7.66
*Ohio State	28	171	6.10	1	2	0	0	0	8	85	10.62
TOTALS	383	1880	4.90	23	5	1	15	0	26	211	8.12
2-YEAR TOTALS	674	3423	5.07	36	11	4	48	3	36	320	8.89

*Rose Bowl

University of Southern California Records Set by O.J. Simpson

	NEW '68 RECORD	OLD RECORD	FORMERLY HELD BY	DATE
1. Career rushing	3423	3221	Mike Garrett	1963–65
*2. Single season rushing	1880	1543	O.J. Simpson	1967
3. Total offense (career)	3471	3269	Mike Garrett	1963–65
4. Total offense (season)	1895	1695	Craig Fertig	1964
5. Most TDs (season)	23	19	Mort Kaer	1925
6. Most points (one year)	138	114	Mort Kaer	1925
7. Most times carried (career)	674	612	Mike Garrett	1963–65
8. Most rush/pass plays (career)	685	618	Mike Garrett	1963–65
9. Most carries (one year)	383	291	O.J. Simpson	1967
10. Most carries (one game)	47	45	Morley Drury	1927
11. Most TDs one game	4	4	ties mark held by 10 men	
12. Most TDs rushing (career)	36	36	Mort Kaer	1924–26
13. Most points (career)	216	216	Mort Kaer	1925–26

* During the regular season established NCAA record by rushing for 1,709 yards.

The two-year Trojan record with Simpson was 19–2–1, including two Pacific-8 titles and two trips to the Rose Bowl.

921
Sim

2910441
C.1

DATE DUE

2910441
C.1

FOX, LARRY
921 THE O.J. SIMPSO
SIM N STORY

02-08-76 C. SHEP HLS

WITHDRAWN

SHEPARD HILLS SCHOOL LIBRARY
9701 S. SHEPARD HILLS DRIVE
OAK CREEK, WIS. 53154